**MACAT**

An Analysis of

# Arjun Appadurai's

## Modernity at Large

### Cultural Dimensions
### of Globalisation

T0272079

Amy Young Evrard

Published by Macat International Ltd
24:13 Coda Centre, 189 Munster Road, London SW6 6AW.

Distributed exclusively by Routledge
2 Park Square, Milton Park, Abingdon, Oxon OX14 4RN
711 Third Avenue, New York, NY 10017, USA

*Routledge is an imprint of the Taylor & Francis Group, an informa business*

www.macat.com
info@macat.com

*Cataloguing in Publication Data*
A catalogue record for this book is available from the British Library.
Library of Congress Cataloguing-in-Publication Data is available upon request.
Cover illustration: Etienne Gilfillan

ISBN 978-1-912302-00-0 (hardback)
ISBN 978-1-912127-31-3 (paperback)
ISBN 978-1-912128-99-0 (e-book)

**Notice**
The information in this book is designed to orientate readers of the work under analysis,
to elucidate and contextualise its key ideas and themes, and to aid in the development
of critical thinking skills. It is not meant to be used, nor should it be used, as a
substitute for original thinking or in place of original writing or research. References and
notes are provided for informational purposes and their presence does not constitute
endorsement of the information or opinions therein. This book is presented solely for
educational purposes. It is sold on the understanding that the publisher is not engaged
to provide any scholarly advice. The publisher has made every effort to ensure that
this book is accurate and up-to-date, but makes no warranties or representations with
regard to the completeness or reliability of the information it contains. The information
and the opinions provided herein are not guaranteed or warranted to produce particular
results and may not be suitable for students of every ability. The publisher shall not be
liable for any loss, damage or disruption arising from any errors or omissions, or from
the use of this book, including, but not limited to, special, incidental, consequential or
other damages caused, or alleged to have been caused, directly or indirectly, by the
information contained within.

# CONTENTS

## THE MACAT LIBRARY

The Macat Library is a series of unique academic explorations of seminal works in the humanities and social sciences – books and papers that have had a significant and widely recognised impact on their disciplines. It has been created to serve as much more than just a summary of what lies between the covers of a great book. It illuminates and explores the influences on, ideas of, and impact of that book. Our goal is to offer a learning resource that encourages critical thinking and fosters a better, deeper understanding of important ideas.

Each publication is divided into three Sections: Influences, Ideas, and Impact. Each Section has four Modules. These explore every important facet of the work, and the responses to it.

This Section-Module structure makes a Macat Library book easy to use, but it has another important feature. Because each Macat book is written to the same format, it is possible (and encouraged!) to cross-reference multiple Macat books along the same lines of inquiry or research. This allows the reader to open up interesting interdisciplinary pathways.

To further aid your reading, lists of glossary terms and people mentioned are included at the end of this book (these are indicated by an asterisk [*] throughout) – as well as a list of works cited.

Macat has worked with the University of Cambridge to identify the elements of critical thinking and understand the ways in which six different skills combine to enable effective thinking.
Three allow us to fully understand a problem; three more give us the tools to solve it. Together, these six skills make up the **PACIER** model of critical thinking. They are:

**ANALYSIS** – understanding how an argument is built
**EVALUATION** – exploring the strengths and weaknesses of an argument
**INTERPRETATION** – understanding issues of meaning

**CREATIVE THINKING** – coming up with new ideas and fresh connections
**PROBLEM-SOLVING** – producing strong solutions
**REASONING** – creating strong arguments

To find out more, visit **WWW.MACAT.COM.**

# CRITICAL THINKING AND *MODERNITY AT LARGE*

## Primary critical thinking skill: CREATIVE THINKING
## Secondary critical thinking skill: INTERPRETATION

Arjun Appadurai's 1996 collection of essays *Modernity At Large: Cultural Dimensions of Globalization* helped reshape how anthropologists, geographers and philosophers saw and understood the key topic of our times: globalization.

Globalization has long been recognized as one of the crucial factors shaping the modern world – a force that allows goods, people, money, information and culture can flow across borders with relative ease. But if globalization is reshaping the world, it is also viewed with increasing suspicion – and it is still not clear how to understand and conceptualise the huge shifts that are taking place. Appadurai's work is now considered one of the most influential contributions to the field, largely because of its brilliantly creative approach to the conceptual problems posed by the deep and rapid changes that are involved.

Critical thinking lies at the heart of the author's approach to his writing. A common tactic among gifted creative thinkers is to shift a problem or argument into a novel interpretative framework, and this is exactly what Appadurai did. *Modernity at Large* interrogates modernity through Appadurai's notion of 'scapes,' a set of separate, interacting flows that, he suggests, cross the globalized world: ethnoscapes (the flow of people), mediascapes (flow of media), technoscapes (technological interactions), financescapes (capital flow), and ideoscapes (the flow of ideologies). By constructing this creative framework, it becomes possible to undertake, as Appadurai does, a brilliant and original investigation of what globalization really means.

## ABOUT THE AUTHOR OF THE ORIGINAL WORK

**Arjun Appadurai** was born in India in 1949 and moved to the United States at the age of 18. His early life in India, his adult life in the United States, and his frequent trips between the two countries, all helped to shape his innovative theories about how people see themselves and each other in a globalized world. In the course of his distinguished career in American academia, which took in posts at the University of Chicago and New York University, Appadurai's ideas have revolutionized studies in cultural anthropology and have proved popular with social scientists who want to understand how globalization affects communities around the world.

## ABOUT THE AUTHOR OF THE ANALYSIS

**Dr Amy Young Evrard** holds a PhD in anthropology from Harvard and is currently an Associate Professor in anthropology at Gettysburg College, Pennsylvania.

## ABOUT MACAT

### GREAT WORKS FOR CRITICAL THINKING

Macat is focused on making the ideas of the world's great thinkers accessible and comprehensible to everybody, everywhere, in ways that promote the development of enhanced critical thinking skills.

It works with leading academics from the world's top universities to produce new analyses that focus on the ideas and the impact of the most influential works ever written across a wide variety of academic disciplines. Each of the works that sit at the heart of its growing library is an enduring example of great thinking. But by setting them in context – and looking at the influences that shaped their authors, as well as the responses they provoked – Macat encourages readers to look at these classics and game-changers with fresh eyes. Readers learn to think, engage and challenge their ideas, rather than simply accepting them.

'Macat offers an amazing first-of-its-kind tool for interdisciplinary learning and research. Its focus on works that transformed their disciplines and its rigorous approach, drawing on the world's leading experts and educational institutions, opens up a world-class education to anyone.'

**Andreas Schleicher**
**Director for Education and Skills, Organisation for Economic Co-operation and Development**

'Macat is taking on some of the major challenges in university education ... They have drawn together a strong team of active academics who are producing teaching materials that are novel in the breadth of their approach.'

**Prof Lord Broers,**
**former Vice-Chancellor of the University of Cambridge**

'The Macat vision is exceptionally exciting. It focuses upon new modes of learning which analyse and explain seminal texts which have profoundly influenced world thinking and so social and economic development. It promotes the kind of critical thinking which is essential for any society and economy. This is the learning of the future.'

**Rt Hon Charles Clarke, former UK Secretary of State for Education**

'The Macat analyses provide immediate access to the critical conversation surrounding the books that have shaped their respective discipline, which will make them an invaluable resource to all of those, students and teachers, working in the field.'

**Professor William Tronzo, University of California at San Diego**

# WAYS IN TO THE TEXT

## KEY POINTS

- Arjun Appadurai was born in India in 1949. In 1967, he moved to the United States, where he has lived and worked ever since. His experiences of living in India and the United States informed his ideas about culture and globalization* (the study of the cultural and social effects of a globally connected world).

- Appadurai's approach in *Modernity at Large* is unique in that, whereas most previous accounts of globalization focused on its economic or political aspects, Appadurai concentrates on people, culture, and ideas.

- *Modernity at Large* remains a key text for anthropologists* and geographers* who are trying to make sense of globalization. (Anthropologists are engaged in the systematic study of the beliefs and practices of the world's peoples; geographers study the world's physical features and the relationship between them and factors such as the distribution of populations and resources.)

### Who Is Arjun Appadurai?

Arjun Appadurai, the author of *Modernity at Large: Cultural Dimensions of Globalization* (1996), was born in 1949 and grew up in Mumbai, India. He sometimes discusses his childhood in his work, referring to his early subjectivity*—a term he uses to refer to a sense of self shaped through culture—as "postcolonial."* India was a British colony between 1858 and 1947 (that is, ruled and exploited by Britain), and British cultural influences still dominated India when Appadurai was a child. These influences shaped his subjectivity, as did the American cultural influences that he encountered later in his life.

Appadurai left India for the United States in 1967 and obtained a PhD from the University of Chicago in 1976. His studies focused on modernization: the technological, economic, political, and general advances associated with Western societies during the mid-twentieth century.

Since the age of 18, Appadurai has traveled back and forth between India and the United States. His work theorizes the movement of people and ideas across borders and regions. He argues that the way different people experience modernity*—the period during and following modernization—depends on their perspective. The world may look different to people living in India and the United States, but they are all experiencing modernity.

Appadurai wrote *Modernity at Large* between 1990 and 1996. At that time, he was working as codirector of the Center for Transnational* Cultural Studies at the University of Pennsylvania. He later moved to the University of Chicago, and is currently at New York University.

## What Does *Modernity at Large* Say?

*Modernity at Large* lays out an innovative framework for studying globalization in relation to modernity. According to Appadurai, Western social science has theorized modernity as a sudden break between past and present. He describes several problematic features of this theory. First, modernization theory* (an approach developed in the field of sociology* in the United States during the 1950s and 1960s to explain how traditional societies could develop and achieve the technological, economic, political, and other kinds of advances associated with Western societies during the mid-twentieth century) implies that "the West" is modern and "the rest" need help to achieve modernity. Second, according to conventional accounts, globalization always leads to homogenization* (i.e. societies are bound to look more like each other as they evolve toward a Western version of modernity). Appadurai disagrees, arguing that globalization and related processes of deterritorialization* (people and things becoming less tied to their places of origin) mean that modernization is not uniformly progressive and homogenizing.

Appadurai believes that the globalized world can be better understood through his own theory of rupture,* that is, the tendency of people and ideas to break away from their point of origin. He suggests that scholars follow him in examining new types of "global cultural flows"* that circulate the world. Migration* (the movement of people from one place to another) and electronic media* (technologies that proliferate images and ideas) are two of the most important flows. Appadurai saw them as major forces of cultural change, especially in the two decades before publication of the book. These flows produce a world full of diverse identities.

Together, the flows of people and images allow "the work of the imagination." For Appadurai, imagination "has become a part of the quotidian [everyday] mental work of ordinary people in many societies."[1] People move around the world and consume mass media, which enables them to imagine new lives and new worlds. This is an important part of modern subjectivity: people are imagining modernity into being, by imagining themselves as modern.

The modern social imagination* (an organized field of social practices through which individuals and communities picture and work toward new possibilities for how they want to live) disrupts institutions that were previously regarded as the hallmarks of modernity. One of these is the nation-state.* Many people now live in diasporas,* communities that originated in a particular place but are now spread out around the world. No matter what nation-state they may now live in, members of a diaspora continue to imagine their homeland. They do so in part through consuming mass-media images that reinforce their diasporic identity. This is one example of how the world is becoming "postnational."*

In *Modernity at Large*, Appadurai calls on anthropologists to develop new theories and methods for studying the world in its state of flux. These should address how global cultural flows work, and take into account how the social imagination produces new forms of subjectivity.

*Modernity at Large* made Appadurai's name as an anthropologist of globalization. It has had a lasting impact on the field of anthropology and is set to become a classic in the field. Google Scholar records almost 20,000 citations of *the book*.

## Why Does *Modernity at Large* Matter?

Appadurai published *Modernity at Large* in 1996 when anthropologists, accustomed to focusing on small communities living in one place, were struggling to develop new research methods that reflected the globalized world. Appadurai argued that anthropological methods should recognize that everywhere is now globally connected. He suggested that scholars examine global flows such as migration and electronic media.

Appadurai's book convinced anthropologists, who were used to treating their objects of study as fixed, to study culture in flux. It suggested that they could achieve this by using models from the field of cultural studies. Many have taken up Appadurai's challenge and expanded their understanding of culture to include the effects of globalization.

Anthropologists of globalization have endeavored to find a

balance between two approaches. One emphasizes how globalization homogenizes the world through cultural imperialism,* a process in which the cultural forms of a more powerful society dominate or replace the cultural forms of a less powerful one. The other approach emphasizes the opposite: how globalization makes the world more diverse in character. Migration and media, for example, are constantly producing new or hybrid cultural forms. Appadurai's text argues in favor of this second position.

Other anthropologists argue that the most important aspect of globalization is its tendency to create poverty, despair, and displacement. Although Appadurai also reflects on the violent aspects of globalization, *Modernity at Large* ends on an optimistic note. Global cultural flows enable grassroots social movements that can combat globalization's harsh effects. (Grassroots is a term that describes social movements organized from the bottom up, through the actions of members rather than leaders.)

The book has been less convincing for people working in globalization studies who have continued to focus more on the economic and political aspects of globalization.

## NOTES

1   Arjun Appadurai, *Modernity at Large: Cultural Dimensions of Globalization* (Minneapolis: University of Minnesota Press, 1996), 5.

# SECTION 1
## INFLUENCES

# MODULE 1
# THE AUTHOR AND THE HISTORICAL CONTEXT

## KEY POINTS

- *Modernity at Large* is a key text in the anthropology\* of globalization\* and has been cited on Google Scholar almost 20,000 times.

- Arjun Appadurai was born and brought up in India and has spent his adult life in the United States. This has influenced his theory that people and ideas are no longer linked to fixed locales, or areas.

- Appadurai wrote *Modernity at Large* for a broad audience in fields such as anthropology, area studies\* (the interdisciplinary study of a particular geographical or national region) and globalization studies. The book coined many important terms still used by anthropologists.

### Why Read This Text?

In his 1996 book *Modernity at Large: Cultural Dimensions of Globalization*, Arjun Appadurai—currently Goddard Professor in Media, Culture, and Communication at New York University—argues for a new theoretical framework, or working methodology, based on the concept of global cultural flows\* (the movement around the world of dimensions or aspects of culture, set in motion by globalization). This concept is intended to help the study of culture in a modern, globalized world.

Appadurai argues that, while previous scholarship analyzed culture as linked to a particular locale, this is no longer useful. Appadurai's framework encourages the study of how ideas, things, and people move

**❝** The story of mass migrations (voluntary and forced) is hardly a new feature of human history. But when it is juxtaposed with the rapid flow of mass-mediated images, scripts, and sensations, we have a new order of instability in the production of modern subjectivities. **❞**

Arjun Appadurai, *Modernity at Large: Cultural Dimensions of Globalization*

around the world in global cultural flows, such as migration* (people moving to live in different countries from the ones in which they were born) and electronic media* (the internet, TV, movies, and so on).

Migration and mass media affect the social imagination*—the ways in which people collectively imagine their lives and their worlds. This leads to new possibilities in how people identify themselves.

Appadurai's insights provided important new directions for anthropologists who were looking for methods and theories to understand culture in a globalized world. The book also encouraged people studying globalization to consider the central importance of cultural aspects of this phenomenon.

## Author's Life

Appadurai was born in 1949 and grew up in Mumbai, India, where his subjectivity,* or sense of self, was greatly affected by the culture that surrounded him: the aftereffects of the British colonization of India, as well as American media and pop culture. He moved to the United States to attend college in 1967 and has been there ever since. Appadurai was married to Carol Breckenridge,* an American historian of India. His lifetime of travel back and forth between these two places helped him develop his insights into the global flow of people and ideas.

Appadurai received his PhD from the University of Chicago in 1976 and has held appointments at a number of prestigious American institutions, including Yale, Pennsylvania, Chicago, Princeton, and New York universities.

Appadurai uses examples from his personal life to illustrate his ideas. He describes a trip to India with his wife and 11-year-old son, in which the boy encountered "many webs of shifting biography"[1]— different ways of relating to tradition, family, and personal identity— among family members with personal and professional ties in India, the United States, and elsewhere.

For Appadurai, the multiple threads that make up people's identities should be the focus of a new kind of ethnography.* Ethnography describes both the method of research and the work produced by cultural anthropologists. Ethnographies have typically been produced through long-term involvement with a locale, observing and participating in the lives of the people who live there. Appadurai argues for ethnographic research that "focuses on the unyoking of imagination from place."[2] As people move around the world, living and working in different locations, how they imagine and experience their lives changes. They define themselves partly through the people and ideas they encounter, rather than simply through their place of origin.

## Author's Background

Appadurai grew up in the 1950s and 1960s. His country of origin, India, was one of many facing the postcolonial* task of building a national and cultural identity after gaining independence. Although British colonialism ended in India in 1947, the country was still dominated by British cultural influences during Appadurai's childhood. However, this was changing quickly as a new postcolonial Indian identity asserted itself.

The quest for a unified Indian identity was fragmented* by the diversity of ethnic and religious identities among the Indian population, with some of these communities stretching across the borders of India into other countries. The end of colonial rule opened up new possibilities for self-determination, so the postcolonial period in South Asia was characterized by conflict between communities and nations seeking political power—and other kinds of power, too—within shifting geopolitical boundaries.

When Appadurai arrived in the United States in 1967, he studied anthropology, area studies, and "that triumphal form of modernization theory* that was still a secure article of Americanism in a bipolar world."[3] Modernization theory was developed by American sociologists* (scholars of the nature, formations, and history of society) during the 1950s and 1960s to explain how traditional societies could develop the technological, economic, political, and other advantages that were at that time concentrated in Western countries. The United States was in the midst of the Cold War, a period of political and military tension between Western countries and the Soviet Union and nations aligned to it. Scholars and ordinary Americans alike saw the United States as the perfect example of modernity,* particularly in contrast with the Soviet Union, which they considered backward and repressive.

Appadurai's early experiences in India and the United States have shaped his intellectual career. *Modernity at Large* responds to American social science theories of modernity and modernization—for example, that modernity was a universally desirable result of Western progress—while the book's discussions of identity and ethnic violence draw on examples from postcolonial India. The book reflects Appadurai's position as somebody whose work and life draw on ideas and images from multiple communities.

## NOTES

1   Arjun Appadurai, *Modernity at Large: Cultural Dimensions of Globalization* (Minneapolis: University of Minnesota Press, 1996), 57.

2   Appadurai, *Modernity at Large*, 58.

3   Appadurai, *Modernity at Large*, 2.

# MODULE 2
# ACADEMIC CONTEXT

## KEY POINTS

- Cultural anthropology* studies the cultural aspects of human existence.

- Although Appadurai is a cultural anthropologist, *Modernity at Large* mainly relies upon the work of theorists outside his own discipline, including the political scientist and historian Benedict Anderson,* who developed a theory of the use of imagination to build community.

- Appadurai suggests that anthropologists can learn from the approach of cultural studies.*

### The Work in its Context

Arjun Appadurai's *Modernity at Large: Cultural Dimensions of Globalization* challenges the methods that American anthropologists were using at the time of writing (1990 to 1996). The German American scholar Franz Boas* is widely credited with being the father of American anthropology. He was uninterested in universal theories of human culture, and preferred long-term ethnographic* research in a particular locale and collecting descriptive empirical* data (that is, collecting verifiable information through observation and interviews, over a long period).

In contrast with Boas and other American anthropologists, Appadurai called for ethnographic research that addressed the global as well as the local. His work was influenced by other anthropologists: for example, studies in the 1970s and 1980s exploring how societies were linked by trade and other international flows.

*Modernity at Large* acknowledges that societies have been

> **❝ [A]** genuinely cosmopolitan ethnographic practice requires an interpretation of the terrain of cultural studies in the United States today and of the status of anthropology within such a terrain. **❞**
>
> Arjun Appadurai, *Modernity at Large: Cultural Dimensions of Globalization*

interacting with each other for a long time through trade and other means. However, these interactions intensified in the 1980s and 1990s because transportation and communication became significantly cheaper than before. People and ideas were able to move rapidly around the world, which led to them becoming disconnected from particular locales. Appadurai suggests that anthropology must develop new theories and methods to account for global cultural flows* and how these flows affect particular places.

## Overview of the Field

Although Appadurai is writing with an audience of anthropologists in mind, his work draws mostly upon scholars outside the field of anthropology. For example, he was influenced by World Systems Theory,* which aims to describe how and why money, resources, and power are distributed globally. World Systems Theorists such as the US sociologist Immanuel Wallerstein* laid out the structure of the relationships between "core"* (developed) and "periphery"* (developing) nations to analyze global political and economic inequalities.

Some anthropologists, like Appadurai, were influenced by the theories of the German political philosopher and economist Karl Marx,* who argued that the conflict inherent in economic systems was the major force behind historical change. They agreed that culture could not be studied separately from social structures and power relationships.

Appadurai added that inequality and power are complicated by disjunctures* in global cultural flows and the work of the social imagination.* (Disjunctures occur when two different flows create conflicting conditions.) Appadurai writes, "[E]ven the meanest and most hopeless of lives, the most brutal and dehumanizing of circumstances, the harshest of lived inequalities are now open to the play of the imagination."[1] In other words, even if people suffer because of globalization,* they still have agency* (the capacity to make decisions and act, in their particular circumstances) in the form of choosing how to imagine new worlds and new lives for themselves.

The political scientist and historian Benedict Anderson also explored the political role of imagination. Anderson argued that the production and circulation of newspapers and books—"print-capitalism"*—helped to create a sense of nationalism* (an ideology expressing the strong belief that the identity or interests of an ethnic group or nation-state are of primary importance), resulting in an "imagined community"* (a group of people who feel that they have an important part of their identity in common with each other, even if they have never met).

Appadurai argues that globalization has sped up and intensified the process that Anderson described. Now the imagined community can stretch across national or regional borders.

### Academic Influences

Scholars in many different disciplines recognized the importance of power and domination in understanding culture. This led them to the theory that cultural imperialism* leads to a homogenization* of cultures around the world. Local cultures would eventually be wiped out, and different populations across the world would become more and more culturally similar. Appadurai argued instead that globalization was leading to the heterogenization* of culture, creating new and hybrid cultural forms.

Appadurai was deeply involved in conversations about globalization and transnationalism (a theoretical perspective emphasizing global connections) during the period when he wrote *Modernity at Large*. He developed the idea for the book while a MacArthur Fellow* at the Institute for Advanced Study in Princeton and wrote it while codirector of the Center for Transnational* Cultural Studies at the University of Pennsylvania. The book was finished during his time at the University of Chicago, where he developed and served as director of the Globalization Project (a group of people working in different academic disciplines studying the economic, political, and cultural links between different countries).

Among anthropologists, Appadurai is known for advancing the importance of the study of global dimensions of culture. This ability to bridge the gap between the fields of globalization studies and anthropology is one of Appadurai's unique contributions.

## NOTES

1   Arjun Appadurai, *Modernity at Large: Cultural Dimensions of Globalization* (Minneapolis: University of Minnesota Press, 1996), 54.

# MODULE 3
# THE PROBLEM

## KEY POINTS

- Appadurai argues for the study of globalization's*
  cultural dimensions through the idea of global cultural
  flows.* He points to the importance of electronic media*
  and migration,* which circulate ideas and people around
  the world.

- Before the publication of *Modernity at Large*, academics
  trying to theorize globalization tended to focus on
  inequality and how it is leading to the homogenization*
  of culture—societies all over the world becoming more
  similar to each other—or else they did not address the
  cultural dimensions of globalization at all.

- Appadurai argues that globalization is leading to a
  heterogenization* of culture—societies all over the world
  becoming more different from each other—that requires
  new theories and methods for studying the modern world.

### Core Question

In the 1990s, when Arjun Appadurai began writing the essays
included in *Modernity at Large: Cultural Dimensions of Globalization*,
he was part of the growing field of globalization studies. While
many theorists of globalization focused primarily on its political and
economic dimensions, Appadurai argued for the importance of its
cultural dimensions.

In Appadurai's primary field of anthropology,* some scholars
were beginning to think about how globalization was affecting
local culture. Previously, American anthropologists had focused on

> ❝ The central problem of today's global interactions is the tension between cultural homogenization and cultural heterogenization. ❞
>
> Arjun Appadurai, *Modernity at Large: Cultural Dimensions of Globalization*

studying small-scale, relatively isolated societies through the lens of holism, a perspective on culture that emphasizes how cultural beliefs and practices function as a whole system.

Appadurai and other anthropology scholars argued against this. They were in favor of new methods and theories that would acknowledge that even seemingly isolated locations are caught up in global cultural flows. Rather than holism, Appadurai and others emphasized rupture*—how cultural practices split off from their origins.

Increasing numbers of people leave the country of their birth to live somewhere else, traveling and absorbing cultural influences from many places. A modern anthropology must reflect that international cultural flows are now more intense and work in new ways.

## The Participants

Appadurai was in conversation with other scholars of globalization who were seeking to answer similar questions about processes of heterogenization and homogenization, power, and inequality. They wanted to create new theories and methods that could capture the processes of deterritorialization* and global cultural flows.

Outside of anthropology, many scholars were concerned that globalization would lead to homogenization, primarily through cultural imperialism.* For example John Tomlinson,* professor of English, culture, and media at Nottingham Trent University, described globalization as "the installation worldwide of Western versions of basic sociocultural reality: the West's ... theories, its values, ethical systems, approaches to rationality, technical-scientific world view, political culture, and so on."[1] The West dominates the world through cultural imperialism, spreading not only Western food, fashion, and language, but also Western world views and values.

Anthropologists generally agreed with Appadurai's thesis of heterogenization and criticized scholars like Tomlinson for painting a picture of non-Westerners as passive consumers of Western products and ideas. The most prominent of these anthropologists was Ulf Hannerz,* currently emeritus professor of anthropology at the University of Stockholm in Sweden. Hannerz's work was similar to Appadurai's theories of the transnational* interconnectedness of peoples around the world, a condition that Hannerz called the "global ecumene."*[2] This term refers to the idea that different societies, economies, and cultures make up one interconnected world.

Hannerz went even further than Appadurai in claiming that people affected by globalization are still able to gain agency,* or free choice, within their circumstances. He described how people living in non-Western societies are "speaking back" to globalization through the process of what he calls creolization:* the mixing of multiple cultural forms.[3]

## The Contemporary Debate

Appadurai argued that heterogenization of culture is what makes our era one of modernity.* With people and ideas circulating the world, individuals and groups can imagine new identities and lives. They can construct these imagined lives around mixtures of cultural forms, practices, and ideas. Appadurai provides several examples, such as the sport of cricket. The British took cricket to India during the colonial* era (that is, at the height of British political dominance and exploitation), and high-status Indians began to play it in the late nineteenth century. At that time, the sport expressed the values of upper-class British masculinity. It is now played by people in the former British colonies and other countries, includes players from diverse ethnic and religious groups, and involves multiple levels of media expression. The global popularity of cricket is a clear example of heterogenization and of the deep historical perspective required to understand it.

The debate on culture and globalization continues today. Other scholars, including Hannerz, have written about migration, media, and other cultural flows. But Appadurai's big concepts, neologisms (that is, newly invented terms, such as "ethnoscapes") and convincing writing style have ensured that he continues to be the major academic voice representing the cultural dimensions of globalization.

## NOTES

1   John Tomlinson, "Internationalism, Globalization, and Cultural Imperialism," in *Media and Cultural Regulation*, ed. Kenneth Thompson (London: Sage Publications, 1997), 14.

2   Ulf Hannerz, *Cultural Complexity: Studies in the Social Organization of Meaning* (New York: Columbia University Press, 1992), 217.

3   Hannerz, *Cultural Complexity*, 256.

# THE AUTHOR'S CONTRIBUTION

## KEY POINTS

- Appadurai's main aim in *Modernity at Large* is to provoke new theories and methods for understanding globalization* through the framework of global cultural flows.*

- Appadurai places an original emphasis on how migration* and electronic media* are producing new forms of social imagination.*

- The book built on previous theories of modernity* and imagination in order to show that the modern world is characterized by new and more intense interactions between people and ideas.

### Author's Aims

Throughout *Modernity at Large: Cultural Aspects of Globalization*, Arjun Appadurai's objective is to illustrate how migration and media influence societies in a world deterritorialized* (that is, where people and things become less tied to their places of origin) through the social imagination. Before this book, studies of globalization tended to focus on economics and politics as the causes of new global processes and structures. The global circulation of people and ideas was seen as an effect of globalization rather than a cause.

Appadurai focuses on two global cultural flows, migration and electronic media, insisting that they are an important part of globalization and a force for change. With the help of migration and media, groups of people are together able to imagine new lives and worlds that were beyond the possibilities available earlier in history. Before modernity, the imagination was limited by the norms of an

> 66 [T]he world has been a congeries [a jumbled collection] of large-scale interactions for many centuries. Yet today's world involves interactions of a new order and intensity. 99
>
> Arjun Appadurai, *Modernity at Large: Cultural Dimensions of Globalization*

individual's or group's community or locale. Today, with access to people and ideas from around the world, people are able to see and imagine other ways of thinking and living.

## Approach

*Modernity at Large* inspired anthropologists and others to imagine new theories and methods for understanding culture. Although Appadurai draws upon past theories from disciplines including anthropology and area studies,* he criticizes their assumption that culture is a specific thing tied to a particular place. This supposition no longer applies to the way people live in the world, if it ever did.

Appadurai recreates the speed, intensity, and chaos of globalization through his writing style. He throws big ideas and concepts at the reader, and rushes through complicated examples to illustrate his points. In this way, he explains two global cultural flows of particular importance: migration and electronic media.

The book makes the case that migration and media, along with the decline of the nation-state,* have resulted in new diasporic* publics (that is, group identities that exist across national and other spatial boundaries). In the third part of the book, Appadurai argues that these flows are crucial to modern movements based on shared ethnic identities, which he refers to as culturalisms.* Powered by the forces of migration and media, culturalisms often lead to conflicts over cultural or national spaces. Appadurai's concept of the social imagination shows how global cultural flows can both create group identities and bring them into conflict.

## Contribution in Context

Appadurai is uncomfortable with theories in Western social science that assume modernity is a universally desired state. He criticizes the way that this assumption appears in modernization theory,* the American sociological theory of the 1950s and 1960s influenced by the pioneering German sociologist Max Weber* and the Frankfurt School* (a school of social thought associated both with the Institute for Social Research at Goethe University in Frankfurt, Germany, and a critique of capitalism influenced by the thought of the German political philosopher Karl Marx). Modernization theory predicted that "the imagination will be stunted"[1] by capitalism, secularization, and other processes that helped to create our global world.

However, rather than stunting the imagination of the masses, "the consumption of the mass media throughout the world often provokes resistance, irony, selectivity, and, in general, *agency*."*[2] Individuals and communities do not simply consume electronic media passively, but use it to build their identities.

To make this point, Appadurai puts a new twist on the concept of the imagined community* discussed by political scientist and historian Benedict Anderson.* Anderson argued that the development of print-capitalism* (national media such as books and newspapers) allowed groups of people to develop a sense of shared identity. In particular, citizens of a nation-state developed a sense of nationalism, partly through reading newspapers and other print media in a shared language. Appadurai joins this concept to his own notion of a "community of sentiment," "a group that begins to imagine and feel things together."[3] This collective imagination, built through migration and mass media, allows people to build a shared sense of identity across national and other spatial boundaries.

Appadurai's argument is original because it focuses on "the everyday cultural practice through which the work of the imagination is transformed."[4] He wants to create a theoretical approach that reflects the fact that people do not simply accept and follow the rules and norms of their social context—they also work collectively to imagine new rules and norms.

## NOTES

1   Arjun Appadurai, *Modernity at Large: Cultural Dimensions of Globalization* (Minneapolis: University of Minnesota Press, 1996), 6.

2   Appadurai, *Modernity at Large*, 7.

3   Appadurai, *Modernity at Large*, 8.

4   Appadurai, *Modernity at Large*, 9.

# SECTION 2
## IDEAS

# MODULE 5
## MAIN IDEAS

### KEY POINTS

- Appadurai addresses three key themes throughout *Modernity at Large*: he describes five dimensions of global cultural flows;* he explores the impact of migration* and electronic media* on how people imagine themselves and their worlds; and he introduces a new framework for studying culture and globalization.*

- His main argument is that culture, rather than economics, should be central to analyses of globalization.

- Appadurai's arguments are broad and sweeping, but he provides several examples from colonial* and contemporary India to illustrate them.

### Key Themes

In *Modernity at Large: Cultural Dimensions of Globalization*, Arjun Appadurai describes five global cultural flows, which he refers to as "scapes"*—mediascapes and financescapes, for example. Global cultural flows are a result of globalization, and influence individuals and communities. Gaps in the relationships between different flows result in disjunctures*—or points of disconnect—that Appadurai urges us to study in relation to globalization.

Two kinds of global flow are of particular interest to Appadurai: the circulation of people through migration, and the circulation of ideas through electronic media. These flows expose people to worlds beyond their original locality or nation-state.* Today, people everywhere are able to imagine "a wider set of possible lives than they ever did before."[1]

**" There has been a general change in the global conditions of lifeworlds. "**

Arjun Appadurai, *Modernity at Large: Cultural Dimensions of Globalization*

Appadurai distinguishes between "culture" and "cultural." During most of the twentieth century, American anthropologists tended to focus on the local and the particular, approaching culture as "some kind of object, thing, or substance."[2] Appadurai prefers the word "cultural" to "culture," because it "moves one into a realm of differences, contrasts, and comparisons that is more helpful."[3] Culture is not a single, fixed thing; rather, we forge our sense of ourselves and the world from a multiplicity of material. Appadurai argues that anthropologists today must not rely on outdated concepts of identity, but should instead account for how people build identities in a modern globalized world. A person's identity does not emerge fully formed from their birthplace or heritage. It is created through comparison and contrast with the diverse communities with whom they come into contact through migration and electronic media.

### Exploring the Ideas

Appadurai begins the book by addressing the question of modernity:[*] a set of attitudes, technologies, and social forms generally associated with Western countries in the twentieth century, which also marks the time we are living in now. Appadurai argues for the existence of a variety of modernities. As people and ideas circulate around the globalized world, differences become apparent. These differences allow people to make comparisons and use their imaginations to understand their particular place in the globalized world.

The title *Modernity at Large* is meant to convey that modernity does not exist in a particular place but is "at large," experienced in different ways by different people living in a globalized world.

These differences result in disjunctures when and where there are gaps or contradictions between different global flows. Appadurai gives an example of a disjuncture in Japan: the country's openness to new ideas and foreign products is at odds with the government's unwillingness to accept immigrants.

In order to analyze these disjunctures, Appadurai proposes an innovative framework for anthropologists and other social scientists. This framework categorizes global cultural flows into five dimensions:

- ethnoscapes*
- technoscapes*
- financescapes*
- mediascapes*
- ideoscapes*

The suffix "scapes" is meant to capture their fluidity within and beyond the borders of nation-states and the irregularity of their form.

Ethnoscapes comprise the "landscape of persons" whose identity crosses, moves between, and influences national boundaries. So Appadurai's concept of ethnoscapes emphasizes immigrants, tourists, and other people on the move. Technoscapes and financescapes refer to the global patterns of technology and money: how they develop and move across boundaries. Mediascapes and ideoscapes are landscapes of images. Mediascapes present visual narratives through electronic media, providing substance for viewers' imagined selves and imagined worlds. Ideoscapes tend to be political representations that relate to national or state ideologies.

This five-part framework examines links and ruptures* among different global cultural flows. Deterritorialization* is a key part of the process, as people, ideas, and cultural forms are moved away from their original contexts and placed in new ones.

**Language and Expression**

*Modernity at Large* is a collection of nine essays reworked from previous publications, divided into three sections. The first three chapters introduce the main themes and arguments and describe Appadurai's framework for a "transnational* anthropology."[4] They argue against previous theories of modernity and for an emphasis on culture in studies of globalization.

The book is intended for those involved in the social sciences and particularly the study of globalization. The rapid flow of words and examples mimics the rapid flow of ideas and people that are described in the text.

Appadurai coins new terms such as "post-blurring" (the modern condition in which already blurred boundaries get even more blurred by globalization) and "gray markets" (economic flows between formal, or white, markets and informal, or black, markets). Some of his new terms have become standard in anthropology, including "scapes" and "disjunctures." He assumes the reader is already familiar with key concepts from the social sciences, and while he provides summaries within each section and a conclusion at the end of each chapter, his arguments are often so broad and sweeping that they are difficult to grasp in detail.

The second set of three chapters illustrates Appadurai's points through examples related to British colonialism,* involving consumption and fashion, sport, and census-taking. The final three chapters turn toward the future, particularly that of the nation-state model in a world of postnational* identities and locations (that is, a world in which the nation–state as an entity no longer exists or is much weaker than before).

## NOTES

1   Arjun Appadurai, *Modernity at Large: Cultural Dimensions of Globalization* (Minneapolis: University of Minnesota Press, 1996), 53.

2   Appadurai, *Modernity at Large*, 12.

3   Appadurai, *Modernity at Large*, 12.

4   Appadurai, *Modernity at Large*, 48.

# MODULE 6
## SECONDARY IDEAS

### KEY POINTS

- An important secondary idea in *Modernity at Large* is that the nation-state\* is in crisis and that the world is becoming postnational\* (i.e. nations no longer matter in a globalized world).

- Relatedly, culturalism\* is often linked to ethnic violence (violence between groups whose racial or ethnic identities give them different access to power or resources).

- Although ethnic violence is the main topic of a whole chapter and other portions of the book, Appadurai's ideas on ethnic violence were overshadowed by his arguments related to modernity\* and globalization.\*

### Other Ideas

An important secondary idea in Arjun Appadurai's *Modernity at Large: Cultural Dimensions of Globalization* is that the nation-state is in crisis. He argues that this crisis is best understood through its cultural dimensions. Because people share identities that stretch across the borders of nation-states, they may no longer primarily identify with one particular nationality.

Culturalism is a related form of identity-building taking place at the level of the nation-state. Nations are composed of people with different ethnic identities, but governments promote the idea of the nation as made up of fixed categories of people. Members of those categories have worked within them in order to access entitlements (government programs that provide benefits to a particular group) or find safety in numbers.

> **❝** I have come to be convinced that the nation–state, as
> a complex modern political form, is on its last legs. **❞**
>
> Arjun Appadurai, *Modernity at Large: Cultural Dimensions of Globalization*

Sometimes this can become transnational,* as groups choose
to mobilize around shared aspects of their identities with similar
groups in other nation–states. For example, many indigenous
groups throughout the world connect with each other through a
shared experience of being marginalized within their respective
nation–states.

Appadurai links culturalism to the problem of ethnic violence.
However, his insightful discussions of ethnic violence in *Modernity
at Large* were eclipsed by his core arguments about modernity and
global cultural flows.* He extended and further developed them in
later works, most notably in *Fear of Small Numbers: An Essay on the
Geography of Anger.*[1]

### Exploring the Ideas

According to Appadurai, nation–states "make sense only as parts of
a system."[2] The actions of nation–states no longer determine the
course of history. Scholars in other fields, particularly comparative
politics* (an academic methodology that compares the politics,
institutions, and conflicts of different countries or eras) have also
acknowledged that the nation–state is in crisis.

Because people's shared identities stretch across the borders
of nation–states, they may no longer primarily identify with one
particular state. Other systems and relationships (such as interlinked
diaspora* identities, forms of religious fundamentalism, or ethnic
nationalisms*) are becoming more important than nation–states in
building individual and group identities.

Appadurai defines culturalism as "identity politics mobilized at the level of the nation-state."[3] ("Identity politics" refers to political views and political action based on a particular ethnic, class, gender, or other form of identity.) He defines the term "culturalism" through a long discussion of his distinction between the terms "culture"\* and "cultural." Culture has too often been understood by anthropologists\* "as an object or thing that groups of people possess."[4] By contrast, the word "cultural" stresses the dimensionality or multiplicity of culture, as a device that allows anthropologists to think about difference.[5] Culture is not a fixed thing but a dimension of identity that only becomes clear through difference or contrast.

Culturalism is the use of group identities for political purposes, often in order to challenge the nation-state. Culturalist movements are "the most general form of the work of the imagination and draw frequently on the fact or possibility of migration\* or secession [regions or groups becoming independent from a bigger political entity]."[6] Appadurai argues that culturalism is the primary form that cultural differences tend to take today and represents a major challenge to the stability of the nation-state.

## Overlooked

Appadurai argues against more prevalent theories of ethnic identity as natural or primordial\* (a characterization of ethnic identity based on strong attachments to a shared biological essence or kinship), instead showing that ethnicity is constructed as a localized response to global cultural forces.

A group is not necessarily born with an ethnic identity. Rather, a group mobilizes an ethnic identity based on cultural aspects such as language, religion, and food. Sometimes such mobilization takes place on a large scale, across nation-state boundaries, or sometimes a group may claim that its identity is based on a particular locale.

Ethnic violence is particularly bloody within the modern nation-state system. Appadurai writes: "The worst kinds of violence in these wars appear to have something to do with the distorted relationship between daily, face-to-face relations and the large-scale identities produced by modern nation-states and complicated by large-scale diasporas."[7] Appadurai's argument about ethnic violence adds nuance to his larger argument about global identity-making and the use of the social imagination.* The social imagination may be at work on a global scale, allowing people to imagine new worlds and new lives, but ethnic violence can result when very localized identities are mobilized across spatial boundaries and come into conflict with the nation-state.

## NOTES

1 Arjun Appadurai, *Fear of Small Numbers: An Essay on the Geography of Anger* (Durham, NC: Duke University Press, 2006).

2 Arjun Appadurai, *Modernity at Large: Cultural Dimensions of Globalization* (Minneapolis: University of Minnesota Press, 1996), 19.

3 Appadurai, *Modernity at Large*, 15.

4 Appadurai, *Modernity at Large*, 12.

5 Appadurai, *Modernity at Large*, 12.

6 Appadurai, *Modernity at Large*, 15.

7 Appadurai, *Modernity at Large*, 154.

# MODULE 7
# ACHIEVEMENT

## KEY POINTS

- Appadurai's groundbreaking *Modernity at Large* added a fresh perspective to studies of culture in a globalized* world.

- The book builds on his earlier seminal essay "Disjuncture* and Difference in the Global Cultural Economy," and provides examples to support his points about the role of migration* and electronic media* in the social imagination.*

- Appadurai suggests areas for ethnographic* research but does not contribute empirical* data from any research of his own.

### Assessing the Argument

In *Modernity at Large: Cultural Dimensions of Globalization*, Arjun Appadurai describes how global cultural flows,* especially migration and electronic media, are allowing people to imagine their world and lives in new ways. He then shows how these new forms can be used to explain ethnic violence and social movements today. The essay was an expansion of ideas presented in his earlier "Disjuncture and Difference in the Global Cultural Economy," published in 1990 in the journal *Theory, Culture, and Society*.[1] This essay is chapter 2 in *Modernity at Large*.

One of the enduring contributions of the original article and the book as a whole is their elaboration of the concept of "scapes"*— of people, finance, technologies, images, and ideas. A group of sociologists in Great Britain, among them Martin Albrow,* have

**❝** As a stimulus to the sociological imagination for current research, Appadurai has few rivals. **❞**

Martin Albrow, "Review of *Modernity at Large*," *American Journal of Sociology*

worked to extend the notion of "scapes" into new areas of research. Albrow writes that the term "'scapes' unlocks a perspective for empirical social research that can do more justice to local/global relations than older notions of community and neighborhood."[2]

### Achievement in Context

Appadurai's "Disjuncture and Difference in the Global Cultural Economy" was one in a series of essays about cultural dimensions of globalization.* Scholars in several fields were attempting to make sense of the ways that globalization had subsequently led to an unlinking of place and people, cultural practices, and ideas, around the world. At the same time, anthropologists were debating whether this deterritorialization* was actually new or simply a more rapid form of the same processes of cultural contact and change that had always characterized human existence.

The field of globalization studies was still largely focused on political and economic factors and often saw cultural change as a secondary effect of globalization rather than a primary component. Through *Modernity at Large*, Appadurai attempted to outline a research agenda for studying culture in a globalized world. One of his major, but most controversial, contributions was his observation that there are new forms of social imagination in the world today, produced by global cultural flows and producing, in their own turn, new forms of identity across nation-state* and other spatial boundaries. Imagination is an elusive concept and difficult to research empirically. The ability of an individual or group of people to imagine new worlds and new lives is a sign that they have agency*—that is, the ability to act and make choices within the limits of their circumstances.

While this idea was appealing to scholars of culture within globalization studies, it was unappealing to those whose theories emphasized the political and economic structures of globalization.

### Limitations

The major limitation of *Modernity at Large* is its lack of foundation in empirical evidence. Appadurai's examples are based on his observations and readings, rather than on methodologically sound research.

At the time of the book's publication (1996), many anthropologists were increasingly critical of how globalization was worsening inequality between people and states. Appadurai's emphasis on agency through the social imagination is sometimes viewed as disguising the constraints on the life choices of individuals and groups.

## NOTES

1   Arjun Appadurai, "Disjuncture and Difference in the Global Cultural Economy," *Theory, Culture, and Society* 7, no. 2 (June 1990): 295–310.

2   Martin Albrow, "Review: *Modernity at Large: Cultural Dimensions of Globalization* by Arjun Appadurai," *American Journal of Sociology* 103, no. 5 (March 1998), 1412.

# MODULE 8
# PLACE IN THE AUTHOR'S WORK

## KEY POINTS

- Appadurai's chief focus throughout his life's work has been to provide and inspire new ways of understanding cultural dimensions of globalization.*

- Appadurai has published 13 books, and *Modernity at Large* is among his best-known works.

- Since the publication of *Modernity at Large* in 1996, Appadurai has continued to elaborate and illustrate the concepts and methods introduced in the book.

### Positioning

Arjun Appadurai's *Modernity at Large: Cultural Dimensions of Globalization* is a collection of essays that he wrote over six years. The book brings together many recurring themes from his earlier academic career, such as consumption, colonization,* and migration.* Most of the chapters are revised versions of earlier published work. The book clarifies ideas about how culture flows through the global economy and offers direction for future studies of globalization.

Following *Modernity at Large*, Appadurai published two works that extended his important contributions to globalization studies. He contributed a chapter, "Grassroots Globalization and the Research Imagination,"[1] to *Globalization* (2001),[2] a volume he himself edited. The essay is an important commentary on the relationship between research and globalization.

The second work, *Fear of Small Numbers: An Essay on the Geography of Anger* (2006),[3] can be considered a response to the

> **❝** *Modernity at Large* remains testimony to the theoretical and methodological contributions that transnational* anthropology and historiography have to offer in an era of globalization and ethnic violence. **❞**
>
> D. A. De Zoysa, "Review of *Modernity at Large*," *International Migration Review*

criticism that his earlier works did not adequately address the negative side of globalization. The text focuses on the relationship of ethnic violence to globalization, an elaboration on themes introduced in one chapter of *Modernity at Large.*

His most recent book, *The Future as a Cultural Fact: Essays on the Global Condition* (2013),[4] is described as a sequel to *Modernity at Large* and attempts to lay out more clearly a research agenda for future studies of the cultural dimensions of globalization. The text addresses similar themes to those seen in *Modernity at Large,* this time drawing on firsthand research in Mumbai slums.

## Integration

Early in Appadurai's life, as a student in the United States, he was wary of theories that made modernity* sound like a universal goal or that associated modernity with certain places. As he continued his studies in anthropology and area studies,* he grew critical of the tendency in these fields to locate culture in a single place or region. Many of his perspectives came about through his experiences as an Indian who had moved to the United States.

Appadurai's work addresses these early observations and concerns. He attempts to define modernity as a fragmented* set of different perspectives. He recognizes that new theories and methods are required to account for cultural change and human agency* within globalization. Using his grounding in theories of capitalism formulated by Karl Marx,* he updates Marx for a global world of complicated identities. He also shows how better studies of globalization can help explain such diverse phenomena as ethnic violence and patterns of media consumption.

Over time, Appadurai has attempted to clarify concepts and suggestions for research made in his earlier works. His recent publications have also answered the criticisms that his big ideas are not sufficiently grounded in empirical* research. He has drawn more and more on his Indian background and used examples from India to illustrate his arguments.

### Significance

Appadurai's work has been highly influential. Although he has now published 13 books and over 90 articles, *Modernity at Large* remains his most important work.

When *Modernity at Large* was published in 1996, the field of globalization studies was relatively new, as were studies in anthropology that took seriously global aspects of culture. Appadurai's early interventions in those fields have ensured that *Modernity at Large* will be a classic of late twentieth-century anthropology. Although Appadurai's later works have been well received and introduced new concepts and methods in their own right, he will be primarily associated with the theories of "scapes"* (the term he coined to indicate the distribution and movement of things, ideas, and images around the world, used as a suffix in words like mediascape and technoscape), disjuncture* (a point of disconnect or separation), and social imagination*—concepts that were introduced in *Modernity at Large.*

## NOTES

1   Arjun Appadurai, "Grassroots Globalization and the Research Imagination," in *Globalization*, ed. Arjun Appadurai (Durham, NC: Duke University Press, 2001), 1–21.

2   Arjun Appadurai, ed., *Globalization* (Durham, NC: Duke University Press, 2001).

3   Arjun Appadurai, *Fear of Small Numbers: An Essay on the Geography of Anger* (Durham, NC: Duke University Press, 2006).

4   Arjun Appadurai, *The Future as Cultural Fact: Essays on the Global Condition* (New York: Verso, 2013).

# SECTION 3
# IMPACT

# MODULE 9
# THE FIRST RESPONSES

## KEY POINTS

- There are three major critiques of Arjun Appadurai's *Modernity at Large*: that it is not based on empirical* research; that it overstates the agency* of individuals and groups; and that it presents a vision of globalization* that is too optimistic.

- In later works Appadurai wrote more about the negative side of globalization but continued to emphasize the agency of individuals and groups in building social movements to address it.

- Although Appadurai intended to reach a wide audience of people interested in globalization, those who have read and debated *Modernity at Large* mostly work in the disciplines of anthropology* and area studies.*

### Criticism

For many cultural anthropologists, Arjun Appadurai's *Modernity at Large: Cultural Dimensions of Globalization* is not sufficiently based on ethnographic* fieldwork. As E. Paul Durrenberger,* emeritus professor of anthropology at Pennsylvania State University, writes: "Appadurai seems to have lost contact with the hard edges of ethnography and lived-in locales."[1]

Appadurai is often reluctant to state causality (the relationship between a cause and an effect). For example, he writes that the British colonial* power in India used a census to count people and assign them to categories of caste (hereditary social class) and religious affiliation. Over time, these categories became important

> **❝** [I]t would be even more interesting if Appadurai himself would take up the challenge to do empirical socio-historical research, using his idea of 'scapes'* in order to show 'the newness' of various cultural changes within the sphere of globalization and, more important, the empirical value of his theory. **❞**
>
> Gijsbert Oonk, "Review of *Modernity at Large*," *Journal of World History*

components of group identity. These group identities have come into conflict, which has resulted in violence. Yet Appadurai is unclear whether practices that count and categorize people such as the census *caused, shaped,* or simply *established some conditions for* contemporary ethnic violence among South Asians. Appadurai cannot clarify his position because of a lack of empirical evidence. Thus, the "rhetoric of this piece is one of persuasion by forcefully stated opinion rather than appeal to evidence."[2]

A second objection to the book is that Appadurai is not sufficiently critical of globalization. For those who see globalization as a system that structurally relies on inequality, Appadurai's ideas about the social imagination* paint an unrealistic picture of a world in which all people and groups are free to imagine the world and their lives in their own way. His insistence on heterogenization*—a process in which cultural aspects combine and change to become more diverse—ignores the ways that government, finance, and labor impose their own order and limit the choices that individuals and communities are able to make.

*Modernity at Large* has not been cited widely by scholars in political science and economics. One scholar notes that "his appealing rhetoric made him very popular among postmodernists."[3] Postmodernist* scholars argue that the meanings of representations and interpretations depend on perspective rather than fixed truths.

This approach has remained popular in disciplines such as literary criticism and anthropology but has held little appeal in political science and economics.

## Responses

Appadurai's work discusses globalization as a crucial feature of the modern world, characterized by global cultural flows.* His goal is to improve the study of globalization through better theories and methods that acknowledge the present conditions of the world, rather than to prescribe changes. For that reason, he seems uninterested in characterizing globalization as either "good" or "bad."

He describes how globalization enables social movements to fight back against its own negative forces. In this way, globalization makes for "a level playing field" in the sense that "when there are solutions to the problem of everyday life, they can be made available to a wider population than was originally possible, and more quickly through the Internet, through other kinds of media, through word of mouth; through travel and through all the methods available through technology."[4] Globalization speeds up and spreads solutions as well as problems.

Appadurai says that his lack of interest in causality is intentional. He writes that "one cannot come to a given situation with a strong prior sense about how the causal flows work. That form is what the word 'disjuncture'* captures."[5] The contradictions and gaps between different flows mean that any situation will turn out to be made up of a unique and unexpected combination of causes and effects.

## Conflict and Consensus

Appadurai uses his own general observations and experiences rather than empirical research to illustrate his points. For example, he analyzes how Indians transformed cricket from a sport associated with elite Victorian-era British masculinity into one associated with fragmented,* contemporary, Indian masculinities. The absence of empirical evidence in *Modernity at Large* seems deliberate. Several times in the book he points out that a particular argument or example needs to be followed up with appropriate research.

In later works, Appadurai directly addressed the debate about whether or not he presents a too-positive view of globalization. In his book *Fear of Small Numbers* (2006), he writes, "Some critics saw [*Modernity at Large*] as presenting too rosy a picture of the globalization of the early 1990s and as being insufficiently attentive to the darker sides of globalization, such as violence, exclusion, and growing inequality. In part as a consequence of these questions, and in part driven by my own longer-term interests, I began to do research on collective violence against Muslims in my home city."[6] This research shows that globalization produces violence as well as agency.*

## NOTES

1   E. Paul Durrenberger, "Review: Anthropology and Globalization," *American Anthropologist* 103, no. 1 (June 2001), 533.

2   Durrenberger, "Review," 534.

3   Gijsbert Oonk, "Review: *Modernity at Large: Cultural Dimensions of Globalization* by Arjun Appadurai," *Journal of World History* 11, no. 1 (Spring 2000), 158.

4   John C. Hawley, "Postscript: An Interview with Arjun Appadurai," in *The Postcolonial and the Global*, ed. Revathi Krishnaswamy and John C. Hawley (Minneapolis: University of Minnesota Press, 2007), 293.

5   Arjun Appadurai, "Illusion of Permanence: Interview with Arjun Appadurai," *Perspecta* 34 (2003), 45.

6   Arjun Appadurai, *Fear of Small Numbers: An Essay on the Geography of Anger* (Durham NC: Duke University Press, 2006), ix–x.

# MODULE 10
# THE EVOLVING DEBATE

## KEY POINTS

- Appadurai's concept of "scapes"* as sites of disjuncture* provided a framework for anthropologists* studying culture in a globalized world.

- Appadurai's ideas on global cultural flows* have been used by most scholars of cultural dimensions of globalization* writing in the last two decades.

- \While Appadurai's work has been used in a variety of fields, from sociology to urban planning, his core followers can be found among anthropologists and other social scientists seeking to understand culture and globalization.

### Uses and Problems

Arjun Appadurai's theory of global cultural flows, as set out in *Modernity at Large: Cultural Dimensions of Globalization,* offers a productive starting point for studying what is distinctly modern about globalization. Many people now share his view that what is characteristically modern about globalization is reflected in the unpredictable movements of ideas, things, and people that he terms "cultural flows."

The majority of references to the text relate to Appadurai's theory that there are five "scapes" of global cultural flows: ethnoscapes,* technoscapes,* financescapes,* mediascapes,* and ideoscapes.* Others have built on Appadurai's work by naming other important "scapes," or examining how these five "scapes" appear in particular locations.

Appadurai's emphasis on the social imagination* was favorably received as a contribution to a longer-term attempt to understand

> **"** [One] seldom comes across a graduate student nowadays whose project does not bear in some way or another on global disjunctures ... In this context, Appadurai's article marks a watershed. **"**
>
> Peter Metcalf, "Global 'Disjuncture' and the 'Sites' of Anthropology," *Cultural Anthropology*

human agency* within global cultural forces. His approach to the imagination draws on a long tradition, dating back to the pioneering sociologists Emile Durkheim* and Max Weber,* and traveling through the scholar of nationalism* Benedict Anderson* by way of the influential French sociologist and anthropologist Pierre Bourdieu,* so Appadurai's theory of the imagination has not contributed to his reputation and fame as much as his newly coined word "scapes."

## Schools of Thought

*Modernity at Large* remains an important book within globalization studies and has been cited almost 20,000 times, according to Google Scholar. Many writers, academics, and thinkers have been influenced by it.

The breadth and vagueness of the ideas presented in the book do not seem intended to start a new academic tradition but, rather, to inspire others to include new elements in existing ways of studying culture and cultural contact. *Modernity at Large* is part of "a long-term project—both intellectual and personal—to seek ways to make globalization work for those who need it most and enjoy it least, the poor, the dispossessed, the weak, and the marginal populations of our world."[1] For example, after later research in the slums of the Indian city of Mumbai, Appadurai wrote about the ways urban planning can respond to the imagination and expectations of impoverished slum-dwellers.

## In Current Scholarship

In the two decades since *Modernity at Large* was published, its ideas and challenges have been taken up by most scholars trying to understand culture in today's globalized world or explain social change in particular communities and locales.

Some have built on Appadurai's work by naming other important "scapes" in addition to the five he outlined. For example, Martin Albrow* and other sociologists in the United Kingdom have developed the concept of "socioscapes,"* or flows of relationships and networks. Albrow writes: "We think 'scapes' unlocks a perspective for empirical* social research that can do more justice to local/global relations than older notions of community and neighborhood."[2]

Other scholars have examined how the five "scapes" are present in particular places. Peter Metcalf,* professor emeritus of anthropology at the University of Virginia, and other anthropologists have found that the concept of "scapes" provides a good basis for understanding the profound and rapid change faced in the last few decades by the populations they study. Metcalf writes of his own ethnographic studies in Borneo that "applying Appadurai's model brought home to me clearly the way in which the upriver world that I knew in the Seventies has been pulled apart by social forces of enormous reach and power, acting not in concert, nor even in competition, but in a kind of mindless cupidity."[3]

## NOTES

1   Arjun Appadurai, *Fear of Small Numbers: An Essay on the Geography of Anger* (Durham NC: Duke University Press, 2006), xi.

2   Martin Albrow, "Review: *Modernity at Large: Cultural Dimensions of Globalization* by Arjun Appadurai," *American Journal of Sociology* 103, no. 5 (March 1998): 1412.

3   Peter Metcalf, "Global 'Disjuncture' and the 'Sites' of Anthropology," *Cultural Anthropology* 16, no. 2: 173.

# MODULE 11
# IMPACT AND INFLUENCE TODAY

## KEY POINTS

- Published 20 years ago, *Modernity at Large* is quickly becoming a classic in the anthropology* of globalization.*

- Appadurai argued that globalization studies must take into account cultural, as well as economic and political, dimensions of globalization.

- The challenges presented in *Modernity* at Large have for the most part been ignored by economists.

### Position

Arjun Appadurai's *Modernity at Large: Cultural Dimensions of Globalization* was published as part of a conversation with others working in the same field, when globalization studies was still a new academic discipline. The subtitle of the book indicates its intention to address the cultural extent of globalization.

Appadurai challenged anthropologists to rethink their methods of studying culture by acknowledging the deterritorialization* of people and cultural practices brought about by globalization. He provided a framework based on five "scapes" of global cultural flows* (ethnoscapes,* technoscapes,* financescapes,* mediascapes,* and ideoscapes*) and the disjunctures*—the points of separation—between them.

For anthropologists, the text is set to become a classic, particularly its second chapter, "Disjuncture and Difference in the Global Cultural Economy." The book is cited in most works on the global elements of culture published by anthropologists in the last two decades.

**❝** [A]nthropologists have essentially handed over the entire business of the future to economics. **❞**

Arjun Appadurai, "Illusion of Permanence: Interview with Arjun Appadurai," *Perspecta*

Although the text has been useful to many disciplines, its major argument for the importance of cultural dimensions of globalization has, by and large, not convinced political scientists and, in particular, economists. Economists generally study globalization from a rational, top-down perspective that is interested in culture only when it offers possible explanations for individual and group consumer habits.

## Interaction

For Appadurai, acknowledging the importance of culture is crucial to economic analyses of globalization for at least three reasons. First, while economic analyses present globalization as a smooth process, cultural analyses call attention to instability, diversity, and difference.

Second, economic analyses often predict homogenization,* arguing that the world is becoming smaller and more similar through globalization. Cultural analyses, by contrast, can emphasize heterogenization*—as people and ideas circulate around the world and stimulate the social imagination, they produce new or hybrid cultural forms.

Third, economic analyses lack a historical perspective, being too focused on individual activity, which does not sufficiently account for individuals as members of groups and communities with deep histories of nation, place, and identity. Cultural analyses can help people studying the contemporary globalized world to "look back" and see the roots of the present moment.

Appadurai does not necessarily blame economists for ignoring culture; he is more focused on encouraging anthropologists to insert cultural matters into economic analyses.

## The Continuing Debate

Several scholars have addressed whether or not economic and cultural perspectives on a subject can be reconciled. For example, the University of California at Berkeley economists Pranab Bardhan* and Isha Ray* note that economics and anthropology "are often seen as extremes along the social science continuum"[1] because of their different theoretical and methodological concerns. One of the key differences is autonomy (economics) as opposed to embeddedness (anthropology). That is: economic analyses tend to view individuals as relatively autonomous agents choosing from the possibilities available to them, whereas anthropologists tend to view individuals as embedded in culture, making choices that can only be assessed in the context of their society.

A second key difference is between outcome (economics) and process (anthropology). While economists are looking for the outcomes of global structures, policies, and events, anthropologists are interested in the complex relationships and events through which outcomes develop. Similarly, a third difference lies between parsimony* (economics favors simple, linear explanations for the phenomena it studies) and complexity (anthropology aims to describe the intricacy of social worlds).

Economics and anthropology ask and answer very different kinds of questions about globalization. Although many respected anthropologists such as Arjun Appadurai, Clifford Geertz,* and Mary Douglas* have sought to undertake research with economists, the differences between the two disciplines have so far made attempts at combining them unsuccessful.

However, some economists have commented that economic

projects suffer from a lack of cultural analysis. Amartya Sen,* an economics professor at Harvard University, concludes that "the cultural dimension of development requires closer scrutiny in development analysis."[2] Culture helps explain the political processes that underlie development projects or prevent them from being successful.

## NOTES

1   Pranab Bardhan and Isha Ray, "Methodological Approaches in Economics and Anthropology," *Q Squared Working Paper* 17 (Centre for International Studies, University of Toronto, February 2006), 1.

2   Amartya Sen, "How Does Culture Matter?" in *Culture and Public Action*, ed. Viyayendra Rao and Michael Walton (Stanford: Stanford University Press, 2004), 37.

# MODULE 12
# WHERE NEXT?

## KEY POINTS

- Arjun Appadurai's work will continue to inspire anthropologists* and other social scientists.

- The book's emphasis on the cultural dimensions of globalization* may take on more resonance with economists and political scientists if anti-globalization social movements become more prominent and powerful.

- *Modernity at Large* is one of the most heavily cited works in the anthropology of globalization, particularly its second chapter, "Disjuncture and Difference in the Global Cultural Economy."

### Potential

Arjun Appadurai's *Modernity at Large: Cultural Dimensions of Globalization* introduces important ideas about how anthropologists and others should conduct research in the context of globalization. Appadurai also introduces significant methodological insights that have proved to be helpful within globalization studies.

Although some critics have argued that Appadurai raises more questions than he answers, this can be seen as a strength of the book that will ensure its continued significance. Appadurai offers specific recommendations to readers on how they can use his ideas in their own research.

*Modernity at Large* is destined to become a classic in anthropology, representing a decisive moment in the discipline in the late twentieth century, when anthropologists were struggling to include modernity* and globalization in their studies of culture. Appadurai's

> **❝[T]he task of ethnography now becomes the unraveling of a conundrum: what is the nature of locality as a lived experience in a globalized, deterritorialized world?❞**
>
> Arjun Appadurai, *Modernity at Large: Cultural Dimensions of Globalization*

emphasis on the heterogenization* of cultural forms helped anthropologists to link the global and the local.

*Modernity at Large* and other, later works by Appadurai have shaped debates about how globalization provokes and intensifies ethnic violence today.

## Future Directions

Some social scientists are building on Appadurai's idea of "scapes." They are defining additional "scapes" where conjunctures* and disjunctures* occur among global cultural flows.* A group of sociologists working with the British scholar Martin Albrow* has theorized that socioscapes* are a sixth dimension of global cultural flows.[1] Socioscapes organize the relationships and networks of individuals within a community or locale.

Even Appadurai's critics still use the terms he invented, naming other "scapes" to show the limits of his theory. For example, the Dutch world historian Gijsbert Oonk* suggests that Appadurai could have included additional "scapes" related to science and the environment.[2] This criticism shows that, even among people who disagree with aspects of *Modernity at Large*, the book has the potential to forge new directions in research.

Appadurai hoped to inspire researchers in disciplines such as political science and economics to consider the cultural dimensions of globalization, but generally this audience has not been persuaded that culture is important in their analysis. However, as Appadurai predicted, transnational* social movements are growing, addressing human rights, women's rights, social justice for the poor, and other global issues. As these movements continue to grow, more scholars of globalization may well be persuaded that culture is important.

## Summary

In *Modernity at Large*, Appadurai argues that scholars should study the cultural dimensions of globalization through the conjunctures and disjunctures between five "scapes," or dimensions of global cultural flows: ethnoscapes* (people), technoscapes* (technology), financescapes* (money), mediascapes* (images), and ideoscapes* (ideologies). He focuses on mass migration and electronic media as two important processes that move people and ideas around the world. These processes produce disjunctures where identities, ideas, and perspectives collide.

Though not based on Appadurai's own empirical* research, the work contains numerous ideas about how others can research "scapes" in a world that is increasingly deterritorialized* and transnational. For anthropologists, Appadurai suggests that cultural studies* provides useful methods for helping ethnographic* research reflect how human lives and ideas are connected across space and time through globalization.

*Modernity at Large* was published at a time when most academic thinking about globalization focused only on the ways it took power away from people. gAppadurai's new ideas about globalization suggest that the picture is more complex, since humans also have agency* within the structures and processes of globalization. As people and ideas circulate and collide, the social imagination* enables people to picture new worlds and new lives for themselves. This act of the imagination, which draws upon a variety of factors, such as nostalgic memories of homeland, mass media, and life experiences, is an important driver of both positive and negative aspects of globalization.

These big ideas will continue to be used to address the questions posed by social scientists about people, culture, and the world system in an age when globalization has, ironically, both reinforced and removed the barriers between people and ideas.

## NOTES

1   Albrow, Martin, *The Global Age: State and Society beyond Modernity* (Stanford, CA: Stanford University Press, 1996).

2   Gijsbert Oonk, "Review: *Modernity at Large: Cultural Dimensions of Globalization* by Arjun Appadurai," *Journal of World History* 11, no. 1 (Spring 2000), 158.

# GLOSSARIES

# GLOSSARY OF TERMS

**Agency:** the capacity of humans to act and make choices within their particular life conditions.

**Anthropology:** the systematic study of human behavior and practices.

**Area studies:** the interdisciplinary study of a particular geographical or national region.

**Colonial:** referring to a long-term period in which one society is dominated and exploited by another.

**Comparative politics:** an academic methodology that compares the politics, institutions, and conflicts of different countries or eras.

**Conjuncture:** a point of connection or coming together.

**Core nations:** in World Systems Theory, the developed nations at the center of the global capitalist economy.

**Creolization:** a process describing the emergence of Creole cultures, or cultures that combine two or more languages, in the New World. In anthropology it has come to describe general processes that involve an intentional mixture of cultural forms and identities.

**Cultural imperialism:** a process by which the cultural forms of a more powerful society come to dominate and perhaps replace the cultural forms of a less powerful society. The term is often associated with the prevalence of American cultural forms in the world.

**Culturalism:** the use of distinctive cultural identities by a group to distinguish itself from others, usually at the level of the nation-state.

**Cultural studies:** an interdisciplinary field of study originated by British academics in the mid-twentieth century that analyzes the idea of culture and how it is created, defined, and used. Although it draws upon anthropology, cultural studies is distinct in viewing culture not as an actual fact of human life but as an idea formed within particular times and places for reasons of power and control.

**Deterritorialization:** the deconstruction of spatial boundaries associated with local, regional, or national identities or institutions.

**Diaspora:** a dispersed population that has a common geographical origin and a sense of shared identity associated with its history.

**Disjuncture:** a point of disconnect or separation.

**Electronic media:** technologies for the production and global distribution of media, such as satellite television and the Internet.

**Empirical:** refers to research or data that is based on direct experience or observation.

**Ethnography:** the research method used by cultural anthropologists to understand culture, usually through long-term fieldwork in a particular locale. The term also refers to the product of that research, such as a book or film.

**Ethnoscapes:** Appadurai's term for the distribution of people in the world, with an emphasis on immigrants, tourists, and others who are circulating globally.

**Financescapes:** Appadurai's term for the distribution and flow of money as it moves rapidly around the world.

**Fragmented:** broken into pieces. In reference to identity, this term indicates the complexity of identity, in that an individual's identity has multiple components.

**Frankfurt School:** a school of social theory and philosophy associated with the Institute for Social Research at Goethe University in Frankfurt, Germany, in the early to mid-twentieth century. Drawing on the work of the economist and political philosopher Karl Marx, noted for his analysis of the role of class struggle as a driver of historical events and for his critique of capitalism, these theorists critiqued capitalism and the process of social development that it had put into place.

**Geographer:** someone engaged in the systematic study of the world's physical features, and the relationship of these features to the distribution of things such as population, resources, and so on.

**Global cultural flows:** the movement around the world of dimensions or aspects of culture, set in motion by globalization.

**Global ecumene:** a term introduced by anthropologist of globalization Ulf Hannerz to capture the idea that people are circulating throughout the world rather than remaining rooted in one locale. "Ecumene" is a term referring to a place inhabited by people who have made it their permanent home.

**Globalization:** a process by which the world is rapidly becoming more economically, politically, and culturally interconnected.

**Heterogenization:** a process in which cultural aspects combine and change to become more diverse.

**Homogenization:** a process in which cultural aspects of different societies become increasingly similar.

**Ideoscapes:** Appadurai's term for the shifting global landscape of political images and representations related to national or state ideologies.

**Imagined community:** a term coined by the nationalism scholar Benedict Anderson to describe how a group identifies as such even though its members do not all interact directly with each other (e.g. a nation.)

**MacArthur Fellow:** someone who receives a MacArthur Fellowship, a five-year grant awarded by the MacArthur Foundation to exceptionally creative individuals whose accomplishments speak to their ongoing future prospects.

**Mediascapes:** Appadurai's term for the landscape of visual narratives moving around the world that provide substance for viewers' imagined selves and imagined worlds.

**Migration:** refers to the movement of individuals and groups from one place to another, either through force or voluntarily.

**Modernity:** a term used by scholars to refer to the late nineteenth century to the mid-twentieth century and the experience of the technological, economic, and political advances of that time.

**Modernization theory:** A school of theory developed in the field of sociology in the United States during the 1950s and 1960s to explain how traditional societies could develop and achieve the technological, economic, political, and other kinds of advances associated with Western societies during the mid-twentieth century.

**Nationalism:** an ideology expressing the strong belief that the identity or interests of an ethnic group or nation-state are of primary importance.

**Nation-state:** a political entity that links control over a sovereign territory (the state) with an ethnic or cultural identity (the nation).

**Parsimony:** refers here to research that seeks the simplest explanation for the greatest number of observations.

**Periphery nations:** in World Systems Theory, the developing nations on the edge of the global capitalist economy.

**Postcolonial:** the period after the end of colonization of one society by another. This term also refers to a scholarly perspective on the aftereffects of colonialism.

**Postmodernism:** a late twentieth-century trend in literary criticism, anthropology, and other academic disciplines involving a critique of the notion of universal truths. For postmodernist scholars, the meanings of representations and interpretations are not fixed but depend on perspective.

**Postnational:** referring to a time or situation in which the nation-state as an entity no longer exists or is much weaker than before.

**Primordial:** a characterization of ethnic identity based on strong attachments to a shared biological essence or kinship.

**Print-capitalism:** a term used by the nationalism scholar Benedict Anderson referring to the production, distribution, and consumption of newspapers, magazines, and books for an audience who all speak the same language.

**Rupture:** a breach or break. For Appadurai, rupture is a feature of cultures, identities, and global cultural flows today, as people and ideas break away from their original locales and come into contact with each other in new ways.

**"Scape":** a term coined by Appadurai to indicate the distribution and movement of things, ideas, and images around the world. It is used as a suffix in the case of words such as mediascape, technoscape, ethnoscape, etc.

**Social imagination:** an organized field of social practices through which individuals and communities envision and work toward new possibilities for how they want to live. For Appadurai, the social imagination is an important part of the new global order.

**Sociology:** the systematic study of the history, nature, and functioning of human society.

**Socioscapes:** a concept developed by Martin Albrow and colleagues, drawing on Appadurai, to describe the distribution and flow of social networks and relationships.

**Subjectivity:** an awareness, or sense of one's self and experiences, that, according to Appadurai, is shaped by culture.

**Technoscapes:** Appadurai's term for the distribution and movement of technologies around the world.

**Transnational:** moving or operating across the boundaries of nation-states.

**World Systems Theory:** a set of theories associated with the American sociologist Immanuel Wallerstein. It divides the world's nations into "core," "semi-periphery," and "periphery" according to their relationship to the global capitalist economy.

# PEOPLE MENTIONED IN THE TEXT

**Martin Albrow (b. 1937)** is a British sociologist. He has published works on globalization and social change.

**Benedict Anderson (b. 1936)** is an American academic and professor emeritus of international studies at Cornell University. He is best known for his work on nationalism and imagined communities.

**Pranab Bardhan (b. 1939)** is professor of economics at the University of California at Berkeley. He has published extensively on the economics of trade, international development, and rural institutions in poor countries.

**Franz Boas (1858–1942)** was a German American professor of anthropology who founded the first department of anthropology in the United States at Columbia University. He is known for advancing the paradigms (conceptual models and interpretive frameworks) of historical particularism and cultural relativity that established the participant-observation method prevalent in American cultural anthropology today.

**Pierre Bourdieu (1930–2002)** was a French sociologist, philosopher, and anthropologist. He was known in anthropology particularly for his concept of the *habitus*, a set of cultural dispositions embodied by the individual.

**Carol Breckenridge (1942–2009)** was an American historian of India and the wife of Arjun Appadurai. She wrote about culture theory and colonialism, and, with Appadurai, founded *Public Culture*, a landmark journal in globalization and transnationalism studies.

**Mary Douglas (1921–2007)** was a British anthropologist associated with symbolic anthropology (the study of social symbols related to religion and food).

**Emile Durkheim (1858–1917)** was a French sociologist, an architect of modern social science, and the founder of the discipline of sociology. His theories on social solidarity and the collective conscience remain influential.

**E. Paul Durrenberger** is professor emeritus of anthropology at Pennsylvania State University. He has made significant contributions to the anthropology of globalization, with a particular focus on labor.

**Clifford Geertz (1926–2006)** was an American professor of anthropology at the Institute for Advanced Study at Princeton University. One of the best-known American anthropologists of all time, he was associated with symbolic anthropology, and produced major works on religion, economics, and anthropological methods.

**Ulf Hannerz (b. 1942)** is emeritus professor of anthropology at the University of Stockholm. He is known for his contributions to the study of culture and globalization.

**Karl Marx (1818–83)** was a philosopher and economist of Prussian origin. He wrote enduring works on capitalism and communism and the nature of historical change.

**Peter Metcalf** is emeritus professor of anthropology at the University of Virginia. He has published works on comparative religion and Southeast Asia.

**Gijsbert Oonk** is associate professor of African and South Asian History at the Erasmus School of History, Culture, and Communication in the Netherlands. He has published works on Indian history and globalization.

**Isha Ray** is professor of energy and resources at the University of California at Berkeley. Her areas of expertise include water, development, and gender.

**Amartya Sen (b. 1933)** is an Indian economist and philosopher who is currently a professor at Harvard University. He has published widely on development issues, for both an academic and public audience, and was awarded the Nobel Memorial Prize in 1998 for his work on welfare economics.

**John Tomlinson** is emeritus professor of cultural sociology in the English culture and media program at Nottingham Trent University in Great Britain. He has written on globalization and culture, and has served as a consultant for national and international organizations, including UNESCO.

**Immanuel Wallerstein (b. 1930)** is an American sociologist. He developed World Systems Theory, a landmark approach for studying the unequal relations between nations in the global capitalist economy.

**Max Weber (1864–1920)** was a German philosopher who contributed greatly to social theory and helped found the discipline of sociology. He is well known for his contributions to studies of economics and religion in Western industrial nations.

# WORKS CITED

# WORKS CITED

Albrow, Martin. *The Global Age: State and Society beyond Modernity*. Stanford, CA: Stanford University Press, 1996.

― ― ―. "Review: *Modernity at Large: Cultural Dimensions of Globalization* by Arjun Appadurai." *American Journal of Sociology* 103, no. 5 (March 1998): 1411–12.

Appadurai, Arjun. "Disjuncture and Difference in the Global Cultural Economy." *Theory, Culture, and Society* 7, no. 2 (June 1990): 295–310.

― ― ―. *Fear of Small Numbers: An Essay on the Geography of Anger*. Durham, NC: Duke University Press, 2006.

― ― ―. *The Future as Cultural Fact: Essays on the Global Condition* (New York: Verso, 2013).

― ― ―. "Grassroots Globalization and the Research Imagination." In *Globalization*, edited by Arjun Appadurai. Durham, NC: Duke University Press, 2001.

― ― ―.*Globalization*. Durham, NC: Duke University Press, 2001.

― ― ―. "Illusion of Permanence: Interview with Arjun Appadurai." *Perspecta* 34 (2003): 44–52.

― ― ―. *Modernity at Large: Cultural Dimensions of Globalization*. Minneapolis: University of Minnesota Press, 1996.

Bardhan, Pranab, and Isha Ray. "Methodological Approaches in Economics and Anthropology." *Q Squared Working Paper* 17. Centre for International Studies, University of Toronto, February 2006.

De Zoysa, D. A. "Review of *Modernity at Large: Cultural Dimensions of Globalization* by Arjun Appadurai." *International Migration Review* 32, no. 4 (Winter 1998): 1073–4.

Durrenberger, E. Paul. "Review: Anthropology and Globalization." *American Anthropologist* 103, no. 1 (June 2001): 531–5.

Hannerz, Ulf. *Cultural Complexity: Studies in the Social Organization of Meaning*. New York: Columbia University Press, 1992.

Hawley, John C. "Postscript: An Interview with Arjun Appadurai." In *The Postcolonial and the Global*, edited by Revathi Krishnaswamy and John C. Hawley. Minneapolis: University of Minnesota Press, 2007.

Metcalf, Peter. "Global 'Disjuncture' and the 'Sites' of Anthropology." *Cultural Anthropology* 16, no. 2: 165–82.

Oonk, Gisjbert. "Review of *Modernity at Large: Cultural Dimensions of Globalization* by Arjun Appadurai." *Journal of World History* 11, no. 1 (Spring 2000): 157–9.

Sen, Amartya. "How Does Culture Matter?" In *Culture and Public Action*, edited by Viyarendra Rao and Michael Walton. Stanford: Stanford University Press, 2004.

Tomlinson, John. "Internationalism, Globalization, and Cultural Imperialism." In *Media and Cultural Regulation*, edited by Kenneth Thompson. London: Sage Publications, 1997.

# THE MACAT LIBRARY
# BY DISCIPLINE

**AFRICANA STUDIES**

Chinua Achebe's *An Image of Africa: Racism in Conrad's Heart of Darkness*
W. E. B. Du Bois's *The Souls of Black Folk*
Zora Neale Huston's *Characteristics of Negro Expression*
Martin Luther King Jr's *Why We Can't Wait*
Toni Morrison's *Playing in the Dark: Whiteness in the American Literary Imagination*

**ANTHROPOLOGY**

Arjun Appadurai's *Modernity at Large: Cultural Dimensions of Globalisation*
Philippe Ariès's *Centuries of Childhood*
Franz Boas's *Race, Language and Culture*
Kim Chan & Renée Mauborgne's *Blue Ocean Strategy*
Jared Diamond's *Guns, Germs & Steel: the Fate of Human Societies*
Jared Diamond's *Collapse: How Societies Choose to Fail or Survive*
E. E. Evans-Pritchard's *Witchcraft, Oracles and Magic Among the Azande*
James Ferguson's *The Anti-Politics Machine*
Clifford Geertz's *The Interpretation of Cultures*
David Graeber's *Debt: the First 5000 Years*
Karen Ho's *Liquidated: An Ethnography of Wall Street*
Geert Hofstede's *Culture's Consequences: Comparing Values, Behaviors, Institutes and Organizations across Nations*
Claude Lévi-Strauss's *Structural Anthropology*
Jay Macleod's *Ain't No Makin' It: Aspirations and Attainment in a Low-Income Neighborhood*
Saba Mahmood's *The Politics of Piety: The Islamic Revival and the Feminist Subject*
Marcel Mauss's *The Gift*

**BUSINESS**

Jean Lave & Etienne Wenger's *Situated Learning*
Theodore Levitt's *Marketing Myopia*
Burton G. Malkiel's *A Random Walk Down Wall Street*
Douglas McGregor's *The Human Side of Enterprise*
Michael Porter's *Competitive Strategy: Creating and Sustaining Superior Performance*
John Kotter's *Leading Change*
C. K. Prahalad & Gary Hamel's *The Core Competence of the Corporation*

**CRIMINOLOGY**

Michelle Alexander's *The New Jim Crow: Mass Incarceration in the Age of Colorblindness*
Michael R. Gottfredson & Travis Hirschi's *A General Theory of Crime*
Richard Herrnstein & Charles A. Murray's *The Bell Curve: Intelligence and Class Structure in American Life*
Elizabeth Loftus's *Eyewitness Testimony*
Jay Macleod's *Ain't No Makin' It: Aspirations and Attainment in a Low-Income Neighborhood*
Philip Zimbardo's *The Lucifer Effect*

**ECONOMICS**

Janet Abu-Lughod's *Before European Hegemony*
Ha-Joon Chang's *Kicking Away the Ladder*
David Brion Davis's *The Problem of Slavery in the Age of Revolution*
Milton Friedman's *The Role of Monetary Policy*
Milton Friedman's *Capitalism and Freedom*
David Graeber's *Debt: the First 5000 Years*
Friedrich Hayek's *The Road to Serfdom*
Karen Ho's *Liquidated: An Ethnography of Wall Street*

The Macat Library By Discipline

John Maynard Keynes's *The General Theory of Employment, Interest and Money*
Charles P. Kindleberger's *Manias, Panics and Crashes*
Robert Lucas's *Why Doesn't Capital Flow from Rich to Poor Countries?*
Burton G. Malkiel's *A Random Walk Down Wall Street*
Thomas Robert Malthus's *An Essay on the Principle of Population*
Karl Marx's *Capital*
Thomas Piketty's *Capital in the Twenty-First Century*
Amartya Sen's *Development as Freedom*
Adam Smith's *The Wealth of Nations*
Nassim Nicholas Taleb's *The Black Swan: The Impact of the Highly Improbable*
Amos Tversky's & Daniel Kahneman's *Judgment under Uncertainty: Heuristics and Biases*
Mahbub Ul Haq's *Reflections on Human Development*
Max Weber's *The Protestant Ethic and the Spirit of Capitalism*

**FEMINISM AND GENDER STUDIES**

Judith Butler's *Gender Trouble*
Simone De Beauvoir's *The Second Sex*
Michel Foucault's *History of Sexuality*
Betty Friedan's *The Feminine Mystique*
Saba Mahmood's *The Politics of Piety: The Islamic Revival and the Feminist Subject*
Joan Wallach Scott's *Gender and the Politics of History*
Mary Wollstonecraft's *A Vindication of the Rights of Woman*
Virginia Woolf's *A Room of One's Own*

**GEOGRAPHY**

The Brundtland Report's *Our Common Future*
Rachel Carson's *Silent Spring*
Charles Darwin's *On the Origin of Species*
James Ferguson's *The Anti-Politics Machine*
Jane Jacobs's *The Death and Life of Great American Cities*
James Lovelock's *Gaia: A New Look at Life on Earth*
Amartya Sen's *Development as Freedom*
Mathis Wackernagel & William Rees's *Our Ecological Footprint*

**HISTORY**

Janet Abu-Lughod's *Before European Hegemony*
Benedict Anderson's *Imagined Communities*
Bernard Bailyn's *The Ideological Origins of the American Revolution*
Hanna Batatu's *The Old Social Classes And The Revolutionary Movements Of Iraq*
Christopher Browning's *Ordinary Men: Reserve Police Batallion 101 and the Final Solution in Poland*
Edmund Burke's *Reflections on the Revolution in France*
William Cronon's *Nature's Metropolis: Chicago And The Great West*
Alfred W. Crosby's *The Columbian Exchange*
Hamid Dabashi's *Iran: A People Interrupted*
David Brion Davis's *The Problem of Slavery in the Age of Revolution*
Nathalie Zemon Davis's *The Return of Martin Guerre*
Jared Diamond's *Guns, Germs & Steel: the Fate of Human Societies*
Frank Dikotter's *Mao's Great Famine*
John W Dower's *War Without Mercy: Race And Power In The Pacific War*
W. E. B. Du Bois's *The Souls of Black Folk*
Richard J. Evans's *In Defence of History*
Lucien Febvre's *The Problem of Unbelief in the 16th Century*
Sheila Fitzpatrick's *Everyday Stalinism*

Eric Foner's *Reconstruction: America's Unfinished Revolution, 1863-1877*
Michel Foucault's *Discipline and Punish*
Michel Foucault's *History of Sexuality*
Francis Fukuyama's *The End of History and the Last Man*
John Lewis Gaddis's *We Now Know: Rethinking Cold War History*
Ernest Gellner's *Nations and Nationalism*
Eugene Genovese's *Roll, Jordan, Roll: The World the Slaves Made*
Carlo Ginzburg's *The Night Battles*
Daniel Goldhagen's *Hitler's Willing Executioners*
Jack Goldstone's *Revolution and Rebellion in the Early Modern World*
Antonio Gramsci's *The Prison Notebooks*
Alexander Hamilton, John Jay & James Madison's *The Federalist Papers*
Christopher Hill's *The World Turned Upside Down*
Carole Hillenbrand's *The Crusades: Islamic Perspectives*
Thomas Hobbes's *Leviathan*
Eric Hobsbawm's *The Age Of Revolution*
John A. Hobson's *Imperialism: A Study*
Albert Hourani's *History of the Arab Peoples*
Samuel P. Huntington's *The Clash of Civilizations and the Remaking of World Order*
C. L. R. James's *The Black Jacobins*
Tony Judt's *Postwar: A History of Europe Since 1945*
Ernst Kantorowicz's *The King's Two Bodies: A Study in Medieval Political Theology*
Paul Kennedy's *The Rise and Fall of the Great Powers*
Ian Kershaw's *The "Hitler Myth": Image and Reality in the Third Reich*
John Maynard Keynes's *The General Theory of Employment, Interest and Money*
Charles P. Kindleberger's *Manias, Panics and Crashes*
Martin Luther King Jr's *Why We Can't Wait*
Henry Kissinger's *World Order: Reflections on the Character of Nations and the Course of History*
Thomas Kuhn's *The Structure of Scientific Revolutions*
Georges Lefebvre's *The Coming of the French Revolution*
John Locke's *Two Treatises of Government*
Niccolò Machiavelli's *The Prince*
Thomas Robert Malthus's *An Essay on the Principle of Population*
Mahmood Mamdani's *Citizen and Subject: Contemporary Africa And The Legacy Of Late Colonialism*
Karl Marx's *Capital*
Stanley Milgram's *Obedience to Authority*
John Stuart Mill's *On Liberty*
Thomas Paine's *Common Sense*
Thomas Paine's *Rights of Man*
Geoffrey Parker's *Global Crisis: War, Climate Change and Catastrophe in the Seventeenth Century*
Jonathan Riley-Smith's *The First Crusade and the Idea of Crusading*
Jean-Jacques Rousseau's *The Social Contract*
Joan Wallach Scott's *Gender and the Politics of History*
Theda Skocpol's *States and Social Revolutions*
Adam Smith's *The Wealth of Nations*
Timothy Snyder's *Bloodlands: Europe Between Hitler and Stalin*
Sun Tzu's *The Art of War*
Keith Thomas's *Religion and the Decline of Magic*
Thucydides's *The History of the Peloponnesian War*
Frederick Jackson Turner's *The Significance of the Frontier in American History*
Odd Arne Westad's *The Global Cold War: Third World Interventions And The Making Of Our Times*

## LITERATURE

Chinua Achebe's *An Image of Africa: Racism in Conrad's Heart of Darkness*
Roland Barthes's *Mythologies*
Homi K. Bhabha's *The Location of Culture*
Judith Butler's *Gender Trouble*
Simone De Beauvoir's *The Second Sex*
Ferdinand De Saussure's *Course in General Linguistics*
T. S. Eliot's *The Sacred Wood: Essays on Poetry and Criticism*
Zora Neale Huston's *Characteristics of Negro Expression*
Toni Morrison's *Playing in the Dark: Whiteness in the American Literary Imagination*
Edward Said's *Orientalism*
Gayatri Chakravorty Spivak's *Can the Subaltern Speak?*
Mary Wollstonecraft's *A Vindication of the Rights of Women*
Virginia Woolf's *A Room of One's Own*

## PHILOSOPHY

Elizabeth Anscombe's *Modern Moral Philosophy*
Hannah Arendt's *The Human Condition*
Aristotle's *Metaphysics*
Aristotle's *Nicomachean Ethics*
Edmund Gettier's *Is Justified True Belief Knowledge?*
Georg Wilhelm Friedrich Hegel's *Phenomenology of Spirit*
David Hume's *Dialogues Concerning Natural Religion*
David Hume's *The Enquiry for Human Understanding*
Immanuel Kant's *Religion within the Boundaries of Mere Reason*
Immanuel Kant's *Critique of Pure Reason*
Søren Kierkegaard's *The Sickness Unto Death*
Søren Kierkegaard's *Fear and Trembling*
C. S. Lewis's *The Abolition of Man*
Alasdair MacIntyre's *After Virtue*
Marcus Aurelius's *Meditations*
Friedrich Nietzsche's *On the Genealogy of Morality*
Friedrich Nietzsche's *Beyond Good and Evil*
Plato's *Republic*
Plato's *Symposium*
Jean-Jacques Rousseau's *The Social Contract*
Gilbert Ryle's *The Concept of Mind*
Baruch Spinoza's *Ethics*
Sun Tzu's *The Art of War*
Ludwig Wittgenstein's *Philosophical Investigations*

## POLITICS

Benedict Anderson's *Imagined Communities*
Aristotle's *Politics*
Bernard Bailyn's *The Ideological Origins of the American Revolution*
Edmund Burke's *Reflections on the Revolution in France*
John C. Calhoun's *A Disquisition on Government*
Ha-Joon Chang's *Kicking Away the Ladder*
Hamid Dabashi's *Iran: A People Interrupted*
Hamid Dabashi's *Theology of Discontent: The Ideological Foundation of the Islamic Revolution in Iran*
Robert Dahl's *Democracy and its Critics*
Robert Dahl's *Who Governs?*
David Brion Davis's *The Problem of Slavery in the Age of Revolution*

Alexis De Tocqueville's *Democracy in America*
James Ferguson's *The Anti-Politics Machine*
Frank Dikotter's *Mao's Great Famine*
Sheila Fitzpatrick's *Everyday Stalinism*
Eric Foner's *Reconstruction: America's Unfinished Revolution, 1863-1877*
Milton Friedman's *Capitalism and Freedom*
Francis Fukuyama's *The End of History and the Last Man*
John Lewis Gaddis's *We Now Know: Rethinking Cold War History*
Ernest Gellner's *Nations and Nationalism*
David Graeber's *Debt: the First 5000 Years*
Antonio Gramsci's *The Prison Notebooks*
Alexander Hamilton, John Jay & James Madison's *The Federalist Papers*
Friedrich Hayek's *The Road to Serfdom*
Christopher Hill's *The World Turned Upside Down*
Thomas Hobbes's *Leviathan*
John A. Hobson's *Imperialism: A Study*
Samuel P. Huntington's *The Clash of Civilizations and the Remaking of World Order*
Tony Judt's *Postwar: A History of Europe Since 1945*
David C. Kang's *China Rising: Peace, Power and Order in East Asia*
Paul Kennedy's *The Rise and Fall of Great Powers*
Robert Keohane's *After Hegemony*
Martin Luther King Jr.'s *Why We Can't Wait*
Henry Kissinger's *World Order: Reflections on the Character of Nations and the Course of History*
John Locke's *Two Treatises of Government*
Niccolò Machiavelli's *The Prince*
Thomas Robert Malthus's *An Essay on the Principle of Population*
Mahmood Mamdani's *Citizen and Subject: Contemporary Africa And The Legacy Of Late Colonialism*
Karl Marx's *Capital*
John Stuart Mill's *On Liberty*
John Stuart Mill's *Utilitarianism*
Hans Morgenthau's *Politics Among Nations*
Thomas Paine's *Common Sense*
Thomas Paine's *Rights of Man*
Thomas Piketty's *Capital in the Twenty-First Century*
Robert D. Putman's *Bowling Alone*
John Rawls's *Theory of Justice*
Jean-Jacques Rousseau's *The Social Contract*
Theda Skocpol's *States and Social Revolutions*
Adam Smith's *The Wealth of Nations*
Sun Tzu's *The Art of War*
Henry David Thoreau's *Civil Disobedience*
Thucydides's *The History of the Peloponnesian War*
Kenneth Waltz's *Theory of International Politics*
Max Weber's *Politics as a Vocation*
Odd Arne Westad's *The Global Cold War: Third World Interventions And The Making Of Our Times*

**POSTCOLONIAL STUDIES**

Roland Barthes's *Mythologies*
Frantz Fanon's *Black Skin, White Masks*
Homi K. Bhabha's *The Location of Culture*
Gustavo Gutiérrez's *A Theology of Liberation*
Edward Said's *Orientalism*
Gayatri Chakravorty Spivak's *Can the Subaltern Speak?*

**PSYCHOLOGY**

Gordon Allport's *The Nature of Prejudice*
Alan Baddeley & Graham Hitch's *Aggression: A Social Learning Analysis*
Albert Bandura's *Aggression: A Social Learning Analysis*
Leon Festinger's *A Theory of Cognitive Dissonance*
Sigmund Freud's *The Interpretation of Dreams*
Betty Friedan's *The Feminine Mystique*
Michael R. Gottfredson & Travis Hirschi's *A General Theory of Crime*
Eric Hoffer's *The True Believer: Thoughts on the Nature of Mass Movements*
William James's *Principles of Psychology*
Elizabeth Loftus's *Eyewitness Testimony*
A. H. Maslow's *A Theory of Human Motivation*
Stanley Milgram's *Obedience to Authority*
Steven Pinker's *The Better Angels of Our Nature*
Oliver Sacks's *The Man Who Mistook His Wife For a Hat*
Richard Thaler & Cass Sunstein's *Nudge: Improving Decisions About Health, Wealth and Happiness*
Amos Tversky's *Judgment under Uncertainty: Heuristics and Biases*
Philip Zimbardo's *The Lucifer Effect*

**SCIENCE**

Rachel Carson's *Silent Spring*
William Cronon's *Nature's Metropolis: Chicago And The Great West*
Alfred W. Crosby's *The Columbian Exchange*
Charles Darwin's *On the Origin of Species*
Richard Dawkin's *The Selfish Gene*
Thomas Kuhn's *The Structure of Scientific Revolutions*
Geoffrey Parker's *Global Crisis: War, Climate Change and Catastrophe in the Seventeenth Century*
Mathis Wackernagel & William Rees's *Our Ecological Footprint*

**SOCIOLOGY**

Michelle Alexander's *The New Jim Crow: Mass Incarceration in the Age of Colorblindness*
Gordon Allport's *The Nature of Prejudice*
Albert Bandura's *Aggression: A Social Learning Analysis*
Hanna Batatu's *The Old Social Classes And The Revolutionary Movements Of Iraq*
Ha-Joon Chang's *Kicking Away the Ladder*
W. E. B. Du Bois's *The Souls of Black Folk*
Émile Durkheim's *On Suicide*
Frantz Fanon's *Black Skin, White Masks*
Frantz Fanon's *The Wretched of the Earth*
Eric Foner's *Reconstruction: America's Unfinished Revolution, 1863-1877*
Eugene Genovese's *Roll, Jordan, Roll: The World the Slaves Made*
Jack Goldstone's *Revolution and Rebellion in the Early Modern World*
Antonio Gramsci's *The Prison Notebooks*
Richard Herrnstein & Charles A Murray's *The Bell Curve: Intelligence and Class Structure in American Life*
Eric Hoffer's *The True Believer: Thoughts on the Nature of Mass Movements*
Jane Jacobs's *The Death and Life of Great American Cities*
Robert Lucas's *Why Doesn't Capital Flow from Rich to Poor Countries?*
Jay Macleod's *Ain't No Makin' It: Aspirations and Attainment in a Low Income Neighborhood*
Elaine May's *Homeward Bound: American Families in the Cold War Era*
Douglas McGregor's *The Human Side of Enterprise*
C. Wright Mills's *The Sociological Imagination*

Thomas Piketty's *Capital in the Twenty-First Century*
Robert D. Putman's *Bowling Alone*
David Riesman's *The Lonely Crowd: A Study of the Changing American Character*
Edward Said's *Orientalism*
Joan Wallach Scott's *Gender and the Politics of History*
Theda Skocpol's *States and Social Revolutions*
Max Weber's *The Protestant Ethic and the Spirit of Capitalism*

**THEOLOGY**

Augustine's *Confessions*
Benedict's *Rule of St Benedict*
Gustavo Gutiérrez's *A Theology of Liberation*
Carole Hillenbrand's *The Crusades: Islamic Perspectives*
David Hume's *Dialogues Concerning Natural Religion*
Immanuel Kant's *Religion within the Boundaries of Mere Reason*
Ernst Kantorowicz's *The King's Two Bodies: A Study in Medieval Political Theology*
Søren Kierkegaard's *The Sickness Unto Death*
C. S. Lewis's *The Abolition of Man*
Saba Mahmood's *The Politics of Piety: The Islamic Revival and the Feminist Subjec*t
Baruch Spinoza's *Ethics*
Keith Thomas's *Religion and the Decline of Magic*

**COMING SOON**

Chris Argyris's *The Individual and the Organisation*
Seyla Benhabib's *The Rights of Others*
Walter Benjamin's *The Work Of Art in the Age of Mechanical Reproduction*
John Berger's *Ways of Seeing*
Pierre Bourdieu's *Outline of a Theory of Practice*
Mary Douglas's *Purity and Danger*
Roland Dworkin's *Taking Rights Seriously*
James G. March's *Exploration and Exploitation in Organisational Learning*
Ikujiro Nonaka's *A Dynamic Theory of Organizational Knowledge Creation*
Griselda Pollock's *Vision and Difference*
Amartya Sen's *Inequality Re-Examined*
Susan Sontag's *On Photography*
Yasser Tabbaa's *The Transformation of Islamic Art*
Ludwig von Mises's *Theory of Money and Credit*

# Macat Disciplines

*Access the greatest ideas and thinkers across entire disciplines, including*

## INEQUALITY

**Ha-Joon Chang's,** *Kicking Away the Ladder*

**David Graeber's,** *Debt: The First 5000 Years*

**Robert E. Lucas's,** *Why Doesn't Capital Flow from Rich To Poor Countries?*

**Thomas Piketty's,** *Capital in the Twenty-First Century*

**Amartya Sen's,** *Inequality Re-Examined*

**Mahbub Ul Haq's,** *Reflections on Human Development*

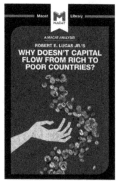

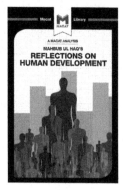

# Macat Disciplines

*Access the greatest ideas and thinkers across entire disciplines, including*

## GLOBALIZATION

**Arjun Appadurai's,** *Modernity at Large: Cultural Dimensions of Globalisation*

**James Ferguson's,** *The Anti-Politics Machine*

**Geert Hofstede's,** *Culture's Consequences*

**Amartya Sen's,** *Development as Freedom*

# Macat Disciplines

*Access the greatest ideas and thinkers across entire disciplines, including*

## MAN AND THE ENVIRONMENT

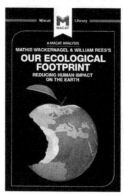

**The Brundtland Report's,** *Our Common Future*
**Rachel Carson's,** *Silent Spring*
**James Lovelock's,** *Gaia: A New Look at Life on Earth*
**Mathis Wackernagel & William Rees's,** *Our Ecological Footprint*

Macat analyses are available from all good bookshops and libraries.

Access hundreds of analyses through one, multimedia tool.
Join free for one month **library.macat.com**

# Macat Disciplines

*Access the greatest ideas and thinkers across entire disciplines, including*

## THE FUTURE OF DEMOCRACY

**Robert A. Dahl's,** *Democracy and Its Critics*

**Robert A. Dahl's,** *Who Governs?*

**Alexis De Toqueville's,** *Democracy in America*

**Niccolò Machiavelli's,** *The Prince*

**John Stuart Mill's,** *On Liberty*

**Robert D. Putnam's,** *Bowling Alone*

**Jean-Jacques Rousseau's,** *The Social Contract*

**Henry David Thoreau's,** *Civil Disobedience*

# Macat Disciplines

*Access the greatest ideas and thinkers across entire disciplines, including*

## TOTALITARIANISM

**Sheila Fitzpatrick's,** *Everyday Stalinism*
**Ian Kershaw's,** *The "Hitler Myth"*
**Timothy Snyder's,** *Bloodlands*

# Macat Pairs

*Analyse historical and modern issues from opposite sides of an argument. Pairs include:*

## RACE AND IDENTITY

### Zora Neale Hurston's
*Characteristics of Negro Expression*

Using material collected on anthropological expeditions to the South, Zora Neale Hurston explains how expression in African American culture in the early twentieth century departs from the art of white America. At the time, African American art was often criticized for copying white culture. For Hurston, this criticism misunderstood how art works. European tradition views art as something fixed. But Hurston describes a creative process that is alive, ever-changing, and largely improvisational. She maintains that African American art works through a process called 'mimicry'—where an imitated object or verbal pattern, for example, is reshaped and altered until it becomes something new, novel—and worthy of attention.

### Frantz Fanon's
*Black Skin, White Masks*

*Black Skin, White Masks* offers a radical analysis of the psychological effects of colonization on the colonized.

Fanon witnessed the effects of colonization first hand both in his birthplace, Martinique, and again later in life when he worked as a psychiatrist in another French colony, Algeria. His text is uncompromising in form and argument. He dissects the dehumanizing effects of colonialism, arguing that it destroys the native sense of identity, forcing people to adapt to an alien set of values—including a core belief that they are inferior. This results in deep psychological trauma.

Fanon's work played a pivotal role in the civil rights movements of the 1960s.

# Macat Pairs

*Analyse historical and modern issues from opposite sides of an argument. Pairs include:*

## INTERNATIONAL RELATIONS IN THE 21ST CENTURY

### Samuel P. Huntington's
*The Clash of Civilisations*

In his highly influential 1996 book, Huntington offers a vision of a post-Cold War world in which conflict takes place not between competing ideologies but between cultures. The worst clash, he argues, will be between the Islamic world and the West: the West's arrogance and belief that its culture is a "gift" to the world will come into conflict with Islam's obstinacy and concern that its culture is under attack from a morally decadent "other."

Clash inspired much debate between different political schools of thought. But its greatest impact came in helping define American foreign policy in the wake of the 2001 terrorist attacks in New York and Washington.

### Francis Fukuyama's
*The End of History and the Last Man*

Published in 1992, *The End of History and the Last Man* argues that capitalist democracy is the final destination for all societies. Fukuyama believed democracy triumphed during the Cold War because it lacks the "fundamental contradictions" inherent in communism and satisfies our yearning for freedom and equality. Democracy therefore marks the endpoint in the evolution of ideology, and so the "end of history." There will still be "events," but no fundamental change in ideology.

# Macat Pairs

*Analyse historical and modern issues from opposite sides of an argument. Pairs include:*

## HOW TO RUN AN ECONOMY

### John Maynard Keynes's
*The General Theory OF Employment, Interest and Money*

Classical economics suggests that market economies are self-correcting in times of recession or depression, and tend toward full employment and output. But English economist John Maynard Keynes disagrees.

In his ground-breaking 1936 study *The General Theory*, Keynes argues that traditional economics has misunderstood the causes of unemployment. Employment is not determined by the price of labor; it is directly linked to demand. Keynes believes market economies are by nature unstable, and so require government intervention. Spurred on by the social catastrophe of the Great Depression of the 1930s, he sets out to revolutionize the way the world thinks

### Milton Friedman's
*The Role of Monetary Policy*

Friedman's 1968 paper changed the course of economic theory. In just 17 pages, he demolished existing theory and outlined an effective alternate monetary policy designed to secure 'high employment, stable prices and rapid growth.'

Friedman demonstrated that monetary policy plays a vital role in broader economic stability and argued that economists got their monetary policy wrong in the 1950s and 1960s by misunderstanding the relationship between inflation and unemployment. Previous generations of economists had believed that governments could permanently decrease unemployment by permitting inflation—and vice versa. Friedman's most original contribution was to show that this supposed trade-off is an illusion that only works in the short term.

Macat analyses are available from all good bookshops and libraries.

Access hundreds of analyses through one, multimedia tool.
Join free for one month **library.macat.com**

# Macat Pairs

*Analyse historical and modern issues from opposite sides of an argument. Pairs include:*

**MACAT**

**MACAT**

### Steven Pinker's
*The Better Angels of Our Nature*

Stephen Pinker's gloriously optimistic 2011 book argues that, despite humanity's biological tendency toward violence, we are, in fact, less violent today than ever before. To prove his case, Pinker lays out pages of detailed statistical evidence. For him, much of the credit for the decline goes to the eighteenth-century Enlightenment movement, whose ideas of liberty, tolerance, and respect for the value of human life filtered down through society and affected how people thought. That psychological change led to behavioral change—and overall we became more peaceful. Critics countered that humanity could never overcome the biological urge toward violence; others argued that Pinker's statistics were flawed.

### Philip Zimbardo's
*The Lucifer Effect*

Some psychologists believe those who commit cruelty are innately evil. Zimbardo disagrees. In *The Lucifer Effect*, he argues that sometimes good people do evil things simply because of the situations they find themselves in, citing many historical examples to illustrate his point. Zimbardo details his 1971 Stanford prison experiment, where ordinary volunteers playing guards in a mock prison rapidly became abusive. But he also describes the tortures committed by US army personnel in Iraq's Abu Ghraib prison in 2003—and how he himself testified in defence of one of those guards. committed by US army personnel in Iraq's Abu Ghraib prison in 2003—and how he himself testified in defence of one of those guards.

Macat analyses are available from all good bookshops and libraries.

Access hundreds of analyses through one, multimedia tool.
Join free for one month **library.macat.com**

# Macat Pairs

*Analyse historical and modern issues from opposite sides of an argument. Pairs include:*

## HOW WE RELATE TO EACH OTHER AND SOCIETY

### Jean-Jacques Rousseau's
*The Social Contract*

Rousseau's famous work sets out the radical concept of the 'social contract': a give-and-take relationship between individual freedom and social order.

If people are free to do as they like, governed only by their own sense of justice, they are also vulnerable to chaos and violence. To avoid this, Rousseau proposes, they should agree to give up some freedom to benefit from the protection of social and political organization. But this deal is only just if societies are led by the collective needs and desires of the people, and able to control the private interests of individuals. For Rousseau, the only legitimate form of government is rule by the people.

### Robert D. Putnam's
*Bowling Alone*

In *Bowling Alone*, Robert Putnam argues that Americans have become disconnected from one another and from the institutions of their common life, and investigates the consequences of this change.

Looking at a range of indicators, from membership in formal organizations to the number of invitations being extended to informal dinner parties, Putnam demonstrates that Americans are interacting less and creating less "social capital" – with potentially disastrous implications for their society.

It would be difficult to overstate the impact of *Bowling Alone*, one of the most frequently cited social science publications of the last half-century.

Macat analyses are available from all good bookshops and libraries.

Access hundreds of analyses through one, multimedia tool.
Join free for one month **library.macat.com**

Printed in the United States
by Baker & Taylor Publisher Services